Emily K. Bates

Kaleidoscope

Shifting Scenes from East to West

Emily K. Bates

Kaleidoscope
Shifting Scenes from East to West

ISBN/EAN: 9783743394919

Manufactured in Europe, USA, Canada, Australia, Japa

Cover: Foto ©Thomas Meinert / pixelio.de

Manufactured and distributed by brebook publishing software (www.brebook.com)

Emily K. Bates

Kaleidoscope

KALEIDOSCOPE:

SHIFTING SCENES FROM EAST TO WEST.

BY

E. KATHARINE BATES,

AUTHOR OF "A YEAR IN THE GREAT REPUBLIC," &c.

London:

WARD AND DOWNEY,

12 YORK STREET, COVENT GARDEN.

1889.

TO THOSE IN CANADA

WHOSE KIND CARE

RESTORED ME TO HEALTH,

THIS BOOK

Is Dedicated

WITH GRATEFUL AFFECTION.

INTRODUCTION.

It has always appeared to me that one of the most beautiful sayings attributed to Madame de Sévigné is comprised in five French words, "*Tout connu, tout sera pardonné.*" If it were not gilding the lily, I would add, "*Tout connu, tout sera compris.*"

They teach us a lesson valuable in all relations of life — more especially valuable in literature, where the character of a country, or of an individual, is in question—namely, that no man or woman can write a worthy criticism upon any subject with which he or she has not some strong sympathy.

A rabid Evangelical clergyman might as well attempt a *Life of Shelley* as for any one to write upon America or our own colonies who is not conscious of some bond of attraction between himself and these countries.

Mr. Froude, in his popular *Oceana*, went to the other extreme, as many think, of fulsome flattery, and *yet* failed to please everybody.

Possibly the butter was too thickly spread, even for colonial throats, or perhaps the general howl of indignation arose, in the first place, amongst those who were unfortunately, but inevitably, left out of the account altogether, to consume their dry bread in the background.

However this may be, poor Froude's name in Australasia is as the red rag to the Colonial bull.

No doubt, in the case of New Zealand, his very pessimistic account of that country's financial state came too near the truth to be pleasant.

Although Froude may have rightly considered it his duty to warn the "old country" of the rotten condition of many New Zealand investments, there is still something to be said from the point of view of New Zealand capitalists who maintain that many investments of a perfectly *bonâ fide* character, suffering merely from temporary depression, were hopelessly wrecked by the wild panic which set in on the publication of *Oceana*.

America is a country which arouses my admiration, interest and sympathy.

I went to the Colonies expecting to have all three at least equally excited, and the result was disappointment; the practical outcome of this being that the months I had intended to spend in Australia dwindled down to weeks.

Australia, as a whole, appears to me, I must confess, most uninteresting; a second or third rate England, with the substitution of a "climate" for our own fogs and bitter winds.

Many will say, "But surely Australia is very like America?" So it is—as a caricature. It has all the "bumptiousness" and self-assertion of America without her originality; all the energy for money-grubbing without her enthusiastic ambition to possess what is noblest in art and literature when the money is made.

I met some few Australians (*pur et simple*) who were altogether charming, and I trust will remain friends for life, but I believe they would be the first to indorse my opinion of the people as a whole.

I spoke to many young Colonial girls on the subject, who were bewailing the too brief Paradise of a visit to the "old country," and saw how much those who had any intelligence deplored the empty, unsatisfactory life surrounding them.

"It has taken us quite a year to settle back into the old grooves again," said one young lady to me, speaking of a late visit with her mother and sisters to England.

"You have so much in the old country, and we have nothing here but sunshine, and one gets too much even of that in the long, hot summer days."

It is not so much the *absence* of art that one deplores in Australia. That is inevitable in such a young country. It is the absence of all enthusiasm for it and interest in it.

"The proof of the pudding is in the eating." These rich people, who will give thousands of pounds to build palaces to live in, consider five shillings quite "an outside price" for any musical or dramatic entertainment. The consequence of this is, that the best artists have at length learnt wisdom, and decline "to go through so much to do so little," as the child said about learning his alphabet.

Mary Anderson lately cancelled her Australian engagement, and neither Irving nor Ellen Terry seems likely to make one. A leading Melbourne newspaper, in mentioning the small success of a really fine *pianiste* who had been giving some musical recitals in that city, added in a patronizing way, "Madame S. is certainly a delightful *pianiste*, but we do not care much about music just now in Melbourne; we have had enough of it for the present"—as though a lame man should boast of his infirmity, or a blind man rejoice that he could not see the sun !

The Boston Quartett Society, admitted to be one of the finest in the world, returned bankrupt from a colonial tour, although I believe a Christy Minstrel entertainment drew large houses at the same time.

The enterprising manager of the latter, whom I came across in Tasmania, boasted of his success to me.

"*I* know how to fetch them," he said. "None of your sonata and Beethoven business in Australia. *It won't go down there.* Black a man's face and give him a comic song to sing : that is the only way to draw an audience out here."

I fear there is too much truth in this assertion.

Mechanical head-work, here as elsewhere, is at a terrible discount. There are only three possibilities open to the fortune seeker :—

(1) Exceptional luck or exceptional shrewdness in specu-
lation ;

(2) Strong muscles for labourers' work ; or

(3) An amount of brain power that would make its *mark*
anywhere, but would rise to the top of the tree here, where
the competition of real talent is of course less than with us.

Mediocre ability seems to fare much the same here as in
England ; that is to say, it pays its way and does no more.
Mind or muscle above par win all the prizes.

Were I a man, with strong physical or mental endowments,
I would certainly choose Australia as the best theatre for the
exercise of them; but I would not spend an unnecessary
penny in the country.

I should practise strict economy during my years of
" exile," and the moment I had " made my pile " should
take the first ship back to the old country.

This, by the way, is one of the prettiest things about
Australians. Even grey-headed men who have never left their
own shores, young men and maidens, all talk of England as
" home " or the " old country."

If a man of sixty who has never previously set foot outside
of Sydney or Melbourne, sail for England, it is always spoken
of as his " going home,"—a little bit of poetry that fits in
queerly enough with the prose of life out here.

And now, having shown by these remarks, taken in con-
junction with my opening sentences, that I am absolutely and
hopelessly disqualified as a critic on matters colonial, what

remains for a thoroughly consistent *woman* to do but herewith commence, or rather continue, her criticisms on the subject?

I shall, however, pass with a light hand over a country of which I saw little, because I cared less, and after tarrying a while in the far more home-like and congenial atmosphere of New Zealand, take my readers with me over some beaten tracks in China, Japan, and Alaska; trusting to the magic of individual experience to shed some new interest over well known scenes.

Every one travels over the whole world nowadays. The unknown in geography has vanished, as time and space seem to be vanishing in these days of telephones and phonographs.

It is not to what one writes about, but to the way in which one writes about it, that an author must trust nowadays for his success.

Verily "there is nothing new under the sun," but every man and woman can avoid being a bore if he or she will speak and write simply and truthfully of what each one really saw or thought; without straining after fine effects or correcting individual experience by the light of what other people *expect* you to say or think, or to have seen, under any given circumstances.

CONTENTS.

CHAPTER I.

CHAPTER II.

CHAPTER III.

CHAPTER IV.

CHAPTER V.

CHAPTER VI.

CHAPTER VII.

CHAPTER VIII.

KALEIDOSCOPE:

SHIFTING SCENES FROM EAST TO WEST.

CHAPTER I.

TASMANIA.

Start for Tasmania—Reasons for avoiding Red Sea route—Shaw Savill line—S.S. *Ionic*—Cliques on board ship—Conversational difficulties—Entertainments on board—Teneriffe, Santa Cruz, the Peak —A mild dose of the Tropics—The Cape of Good Hope, Table Rock, and the Twelve Apostles—Rough weather at sea—Accidents on board—Poor Jonah!—Arrival in Hobart Town—Difficulties of a sea captain's life—A new career suggested for superannuated captains—Mount Wellington—Agricultural possibilities of Tasmania —Absence of men—Social life—" Hen Conventions "—Small-pox outbreak—A honeymoon in quarantine—The domain—Botanical Gardens—Exquisite flowers—A trip to New Norfolk—Salmon preserves—Gorgeous birds—On the Huon River—Tasmanian coal— Franklin—An enterprising young woman—An intelligent jeweller —Hobart Cathedral—A subtle sermon—Sir John Franklin *In Memoriam*.

HAVING made up my mind to join the friend with whom I had previously travelled in America, in the Australasian Colonies, I took passage to Hobart, Tasmania, in one of the two direct lines which ply between London, Plymouth, and

a.

B

New Zealand; touching at Teneriffe, the Cape of Good Hope, and Hobart *en route.*

My reason for avoiding the more popular line by the Suez Canal lay in the time of year when I was leaving England.

It seemed to me that the Red Sea in the month of August must suggest a very "thin sheet of tissue paper" between ourselves and the infernal regions.

There is in fact one ghastly story told (and I have reason to know, an authentic one) of a certain voyage made by one of the Orient line of steamers, when no less than *nine* unfortunate men and women (including the doctor) succumbed to the terrible heat of the Red Sea in that month.

This no doubt was a very exceptional case. Still it seemed wiser to be upon the safe side, and I had no reason to regret my choice of the "Shaw, Savill and Albion" line, or the Fate which carried me on board the *Ionic,* one of the three steamers chartered by that line from the White Star Company.

Curiously enough—from the bad sailor point of view—this second experience of a White Star steamer, landed me after "forty-two days out" with a perfect immunity from sea-sickness.

Of the voyage itself, I must confess that my recollections are scarcely rose-tinted, in spite of this lucky escape. Cliques are doubtless the invariable and inevitable result of a long sea-voyage. In fact, any old traveller, gifted with observation, who has been on board ship even for a week, will be able to gauge pretty accurately the probable "fortuitous combination of atoms of humanity."

Some trifle—the choice of a seat at dinner, the position of a deck chair next to your own, some small civility exchanged with a fellow passenger—will suffice to begin an acquaintance which may develop into a friendship, and is pretty sure to form the nucleus of a clique. Emerging after breakfast, one naturally foregathers with those to whom one has already spoken; walks the deck with them and sits near them, when the tropical heat makes walking a nuisance.

A few more, perchance, are added to the charmed circle, and so the much-abused "clique" is formed, and one's companionship for the voyage becomes a *fait accompli*. Judicious travellers will always take care to make their deck acquaintances apart from those who sit near them in the dining-saloon, or they will find a forty-two days' voyage too crucial a test of their conversational powers. It is quite difficult enough to find material for a hundred and forty-six meals, without providing "deck padding" in addition to this.

I remember a dear old lady friend of mine, spending some months in a Roman *pension*, where she had been given the place of honour next to the lady of the house, requested at last to be allowed to go down to the bottom of the table and work her way up again, so as to relieve them both from the perpetual *rechauffé* of old subjects of conversation.

It seemed to me a daring but grand idea, and might be imitated with advantage on many ocean trips to the relief of all parties concerned.

I should suggest a sort of "general post" every week, and think this would go far to break up some of the too solid lumps of ship society.

The only practical drawback lies in the question of stewards' "tips," but this could be easily arranged through a general dinner and breakfast fund, to be equally divided at the end of the voyage.

Although "cliques" on board are inevitable, still there are cliques and cliques.

Because you find special sympathy with certain human beings in a crowd and prefer their society, it is surely not necessary to glare at the rest of the world as though their very existence were an insult to you; nor to ignore the courtesies and amenities of life, endeavouring to monopolize for yourselves or your friends the best of everything that may be going in the way of the most comfortable seats at the various entertainments or the most prominent "parts" in those entertainments.

It is this absence of the courtesy which marks the conduct of well-bred people towards each other, and upon which society hangs, that accounts for much of the heart-burning and many of the disagreeables attending a long voyage with a mixed company.

Ours was almost exclusively a "colonial mixture," and

the behaviour of its component parts did not tend to bias one in favour of the country beforehand. Here, as everywhere else, the men of course have the best of it. A man can take shelter from the strife of feminine tongues, in that city of refuge, the "smoking-room," and there philosophize at his ease over the small wars that may be raging down below, even though his own womankind should be foremost in the fray.

Our kind and genial captain certainly did his best to "resolve" all the discords, and draw the canopy of peace around the whole thirty first-class passengers, but his efforts scarcely met with deserved success.

For the first week, I struggled manfully against the tide, endeavouring to be pleasant and genial to everybody. After that, I recognized the hopelessness of the attempt, and floated with the "English contingent"—almost the only two thorough gentlewomen in our saloon.

When entertainments, musical, dancing, or dramatic, are given on board these ocean steamers, it is customary for the first and second saloon passengers to send reciprocal invitations, and I thought that we might have taken many a lesson in good manners from the latter.

When we gave a concert in our saloon, there seemed to be a general scramble amongst us for the best seats; whilst our second-class guests were allowed to wander in unwelcomed, and seat themselves as best they might, and often in very inferior places.

When *they* gave an entertainment, all the best seats were left unoccupied until our arrival; one of the gentlemen stood at the entrance to the saloon to receive and welcome us, and show us to the best places at his disposal. Surely a practical reminder that money and good manners are oftentimes divorced!

Having left Plymouth on Saturday, August 13th, we sighted Teneriffe about 6 A.M. on Thursday, August 18th. Unfortunately, Santa Cruz, where we dropped anchor, is the least beautiful part of the island. Orotave, which has become of late years so popular a health resort, is some miles from the port, a hilly and beautiful drive over to the other 'side of the island.

We landed in small boats, which rocked and tossed in a way to make one appreciate the calm start from Plymouth and the apparent immovability of the *Ionic*. Alas! appearances are deceitful! Later we became well acquainted with the rolling powers of our "steady old steamer!"

At Teneriffe we breakfasted at a small hotel, walked through a hot baking little square, and a dull little hilly town, where ironmongers and basket and straw hat makers seemed to "divide the honours" of manufacture.

The public garden looked mournful and deserted, but a few pretty tropical plants and shrubs held up their heads in defiance of dust and heat, and brightened the scene.

Our few passengers for Orotave were quickly disembarked, some provisions taken in, and we returned to our ship with the curious feeling of relief that one experiences on similar occasions after a few hot tiring hours on shore.

Steaming out of the harbour at noon, we had a grand view of the famous Peak of Teneriffe looming high above our heads, and so once more out at sea, and Heigh ho for the Tropics!

I must say the Tropics treated us very well on this occasion. We had certainly four or five days of uncomfortable heat, when the daily walks were abandoned, and deck chairs were at a premium, but out of the eight days within this region two or three were positively cool, and I had good reason to congratulate myself on the choice of route.

On Tuesday, September 4th, we sighted the Cape of Good Hope, every passenger on board being up at 6 A.M. or earlier, to watch this most interesting coast-line.

The curiously-shaped mountains known as the " Lion's Head," the " Twelve Apostles," &c., were in turn recognized as we steamed into the bay, whilst high above the town towered the famous Table Rock, whose outline on this perfect summer's morning lay clear and sharp against a cloudless blue sky.

Few are so fortunate as we were, in seeing this curious rock to advantage, for it is generally enveloped in clouds and mist.

Cape Town lies in horse-shoe form round the bay, and under shelter of this rock, and must be extremely hot and relaxing in consequence.

Far away on the opposite coast stretches the beautiful deep blue, mysterious-looking range of the Kimberley Mountains, losing itself in the dim, dim distance.

This also is the road to the Diamond Mines, and to the famous Weinberg, whence comes the Costantia wine. Unfortunately we had not time to take this drive, which occupies from four to five hours.

So we engaged some very shady-looking hansom cabs, and drove round the dusty hot colonial town, on the Kluft Road.

Sunday seems to be strictly observed here, so the town was empty and forsaken, and we saw little of interest, except some women dressed in grand yellow and green silk dresses with enormous crinolines.

The population appeared to be a motley collection of Dutch Boers, Hottentots, and English.

The "west end" of Cape Town consists of some pretty villa-like houses, stretching far away to the left, as you face the harbour from the town.

The heat on the morning of our visit was intense, although it was only spring-time here. If the summer heat is in any sort of proportion to it, it must be unbearable. I find, however, that the seasons are almost as variable and changeable out here as in Old England, and the experience of one year seems no criterion for the next.

Returning to our ship about noon, we sailed for Hobart, eighteen or nineteen days without further sight of land.

After leaving the Cape the weather became rough, cold, and dreary. The constant rolling of the ship is most irritating and trying to the nerves, even when it has no worse results.

To perform a sort of impromptu "sword dance" amongst bags and portmanteaus in your cabin three or four times a day does not tend to raise the spirits or calm the nerves.

White suits, straw hats, tropical garments in general were laid aside, and every available rug and wrap produced. It is difficult to make people believe or remember that nearly every sea-voyage has a greater proportion of cold than hot days. Nothing is more difficult than to realize when you are very hot that you will ever again feel very cold, and consequently many people who should know better, start ill prepared to meet the biting winds that are sure to come before the voyage is ended.

Four or five little unprotected children, going to Hobart under charge of the second saloon stewardess, suffered terribly in this way, and would have suffered more had this kind woman not begged and borrowed flannels and shawls from the passengers in their behalf.

They were being sent on to join their father and mother (the former an English officer) in Tasmania, and I suppose the relations who packed them off must have had rather vague geographical notions. Probably they had heard that Hobart had a fine warm climate, and never remembered the bitter cold of the very southerly route taken by this direct line of steamers.

It was very quaint to see the youngest of the flock, a sweet, dark-eyed little witch of four years old, trailing about the deck in a "grown-up" Shetland shawl which made quite a long train for her. She was the pet and darling of the whole ship, and a terrible little flirt withal, but we all succumbed to the witchery of her dark eyes and the bribery of her kisses.

Even our most stiff and pompous old Colonial (a very mine of wealth if you could buy him at your price and sell him at his own) unbent when this tiny sorceress clambered on his knee, and I actually heard him one day giving her a true and faithful account of the "little pigs going to market."

The old gentleman had been somewhat of a "gay Lothario" in younger days, and lived upon this reputation, taking great pains to hide the dilapidations of Time under a very lively and devoted manner to the fair sex. So it was rather hard upon him, when the little puss, in return for the history of the pigs, put one caressing tiny hand upon the old beau's few remaining grey hairs, and said, in a patronizing way, " *Your hair is beginning to grow !* "

This voyage brought the usual casualties when the rough weather had fairly set in. One afternoon was especially disastrous. One young lady was thrown violently down against the bulwarks by a tremendous wave, having her cheek cut completely open just below the line of the eye. A lady's maid was knocked down by the same wave, but escaped with a severe sprain; and a young man standing near them also fell, and was badly strained in the back.

There seems to be a special Providence over children on board ship, but one little girl of five years old had her head cut open by tumbling down the "companion way," one evening when we were all sitting quietly at dinner.

By far the saddest and most serious catastrophe, however, happened to a young Scotch lady on her way to New Zealand to help a married brother and his wife in bringing up a large young family. Paralysis of the optic nerve came on quite suddenly one afternoon, a fortnight after leaving England; and for the rest of the voyage she had to remain a prisoner in her cabin, with eyes thickly bandaged, and the "dead light" fastened down day and night. Of course we took it in turns to try and relieve the tedium of her existence under these distressing circumstances, but talking in pitch darkness is not an easy matter, and those who are sensitive to "atmospheres" will find their conversational powers at a very low ebb if they are ever forced to make the experiment.

The weather continued so determinedly rough and bad that we began to look with suspicion upon the only cleric on board—a very harmless young curate, going out to the colonies for two years in search of health—who gained the sobriquet of "Jonah" by resenting so deeply the captain's time-honoured joke, of being on the look-out for a whale to devour him, if the waves were not soon "ruled a little straighter."

Poor Jonah! He was a most kind-hearted and conscientious man, in spite of some little peculiarities, and an overflowing sense of the importance of the priesthood.

It was with real sorrow that I learned some months later that he had fallen a victim to typhoid fever contracted at Melbourne. He died in the general hospital at Dunedin in New Zealand, without one creature near who knew anything of him. The curiously unfortunate part of the business being that I was actually in Dunedin at the time he lay there so ill, and was spending a day with the Bishop; but by some ill chance did not happen to speak of the hospital, nor hear that a fellow countryman and fellow passenger was dying there.

On the early morning of September 23rd, we sighted at last, the Tasmanian coast having been delayed two days by the strong head winds we had encountered.

Tasmania has a most beautiful, broken up coast-line, and our binoculars were in constant request all day long as we rounded the island, steaming up Storm Bay by the Iron Pot Lighthouse, to the mouth of the Derwent and the Bay of Hobart.

Unfortunately we did not cast anchor till 9 P.M., when darkness had come on, and so we missed the beautiful approach through the harbour. To the New Zealand passengers, who would have no later opportunity of seeing the harbour, the loss was specially aggravating.

As I was travelling alone to join my friend, the captain had taken me under his kindly care, and promised to see me safely landed. So I let the other passengers for Tasmania land alone, with the eye of faith firmly fixed upon the captain's cabin. Arriving in port means a very busy time for the head of the ship—pilot and agents to be interviewed, innumerable letters to be written and despatched, orders to be given, instructions to be received. It seems to me that a captain requires eyes all round his head, and an extra pair of hands to get through all he has to do, and often in such limited time.

After a wide experience, I have come to the conclusion that to be captain of one of these important lines of ocean steamers is to hold about as difficult a " hand " as can be dealt to one in the game of life. A man who has the enthusiasm of his calling and an unquenchable love of the ocean may find some compensation in these, but on the whole the life must be extremely monotonous, whilst the responsibilities and possible worries and disagreeable risks (apart from risk of life) seem to me out of all proportion to the rewards offered.

If things go wrong, the captain is abused. If one passenger plays practical jokes upon another, the latter "complains to the captain."

When the men quarrel in the smoking-room, or the women in the saloon, the captain is expected to lend a sympathetic ear to the tale of woe from either side.

If he speak more to one lady than another, the rest resent it; or, worse still, some *man* (who probably would like to be in his place) resents it still more strongly, and possibly lays a formal complaint before the owners of the ship.

If the captain happens to be musical, and offers to sing or play for the entertainment of the passengers, there are always grumblers, who "wish to goodness he would stick to his business, and remember he is there to navigate the ship and not to amuse or trouble his head about the passengers."

If, on the contrary, he leaves them entirely to their own devices, " he is a selfish old bear, and Captain —— of the —— was fifty times pleasanter; and they will never sail in *his* ship again."

The character of the captain of one of these large ships is as fragile and as easily tarnished as that of a woman, or a clergyman.

Once let him become unpopular, and his employers grow dissatisfied. The most trivial and unjust complaints will then receive a hearing, and the risk of loss of employment may stare a man in the face at any moment after years of honest and devoted service in the interest of any given line. No doubt this is looking on the dark side of the picture, but the shadows exist and are very real.

To be a dissenting minister at the mercy of a carping congregation doubtless is equally risky, and certainly there is one avenue open to the captain if he be a man of any literary ability. A long life of observation on a passenger steamer should be a glorious school in which to graduate as a novelist. The *dramatis personæ* are there ready to hand, constantly passing before his eyes in ever-shifting combinations; whilst the whole play is changed, and an entirely new programme published, at least three or four times a year.

Hobart, or Hobart Town as it is more correctly called, is beautifully situated on a tongue of land running straight down to the bay between a long range of hills on either side. The snow-capped peaks of Mount Wellington (4,000 to 5,000 feet high) rise behind the town, and form one of the most striking features of the landscape.

The town itself is small, sleepy, colonial, and unfinished looking, but many of the houses are of stone, and there are some fine buildings amongst them.

The cathedral, as also the new deanery, is built of stone, and when the nave is finished, and a spire or tower added, will look very imposing.

The Dean of Hobart (Dundas) and his hospitable wife told me much of the life at present going on in "Sleepy

Hollow," as it is called, and through their kindness I was able to meet many of the present inhabitants.

The prospects of Tasmania seem rather gloomy just now, and trade is said to be at a very low ebb. The palmy days of the colony died out when the convict station of Port Arthur was abolished. Before that time, Government money to the amount of from £1,000 to £2,000 a week was spent here, whereas nowadays half the tradesmen seem to be bankrupt.

One of the most noticeable characteristics of Hobart is the almost total "extinction of man" there. I suppose sons are born to Tasmanian fathers and mothers as to other people, but they must leave their native island very early, and doubtless drift into the wider stream of Australian life, which is close at hand for them.

And so the evil acts and reacts: commercial depression sends the youth and energy out of the colony to find more congenial soil elsewhere, and the absence of young and enterprising blood increases the depression in trade.

Tasmania is so gifted in climate, and rich in natural productions of the soil, that one can only trust some fresh impetus may be given to its agricultural trade at any rate. Moreover, this gifted island possesses in Mount Bischoff the biggest tin mine in the world.

Vast quantities of fruit, especially of plums and apples, are sent hence yearly to New Zealand and Australia, and this beautiful island might become a fruit and vegetable garden on a very large scale, for its surrounding colonial neighbours, if sufficient inducement could be given to the sons of the soil to remain and till it, instead of emigrating elsewhere in search of a quicker road to wealth.

This fact of the enormous majority of women over men struck me very forcibly at various "at homes" which I attended during a three or four weeks' detention in Hobart, owing to small-pox having broken out in Launceston the day after I landed. I have often counted from forty to fifty women, many of them young and pretty, to a proportion of *three* men, of whom one would probably be the host.

The lamentable social consequence of this is to make the matrimonial market as "tight" here as it is at home; and one hears quite as much of scheming mothers, designing daughters, and "run after young men." These latter must have a very good time in Tasmanian society, but Nemesis no doubt is upon them during January and February, when Hobart wakes up to a brief "midsummer madness." Then the harbour is full of ships, men-of-war, bringing middies and lieutenants in their train. The hotels drive a short but thriving trade. The boarding-houses are full to overflowing, and no doubt the Tasmanian young ladies indemnify themselves by judicious flirtations with their numerous admirers for the humiliations of the past.

There are some beautiful excursions to be made within twenty or thirty miles of Hobart, but few people remain long

enough to see more than the beautiful harbour, and perhaps
Fern Hollow, a lovely dell within four miles of the town, where
many get their first glimpse of the exquisite tree ferns so
universal in Australia, and one of the chief redeeming
points of that colony.

Small-pox is naturally dreaded out here, where as yet it
has made comparatively little progress, and the quarantine
regulations both in Australia and New Zealand became so
strict when the first rumours of the disease in Tasmania
spread that we were virtually kept prisoners there as hopelessly as the convicts of old. For who would care to take ship
for Melbourne or Sydney, with the prospect of a fortnight in
quarantine in one or other harbour, even allowing that the
disease itself did not break out on board?

I knew one enterprising bride and bridegroom who had
been married in Melbourne the day before I reached
Tasmania, and had come thither for their honeymoon. The
husband was employed in some large business house in
Melbourne, and his days were numbered, so he and his wife
actually sailed into quarantine to spend the last fortnight of
their honeymoon, rather than wait for the chance of the
quarantine being raised. It would at least show his employers that he had done his best to return to his duties.
Surely such zeal and conscientiousness deserved a better
reward than a quarantine honeymoon!

There is a bright side to most misfortunes, and the
small-pox outbreak which, after all, was mercifully limited

and soon suppressed, gave me the opportunity of seeing much more of Tasmania than I should otherwise have done.

The "Domain," a beautiful stretch of park-like ground where the Governor's house is situated, slopes down to the lovely Botanical Gardens, where trees, shrubs, and flowers grow in a profusion and size unequalled in my experience since Californian days of travel.

Some of the cinerarias measured two inches in diameter. Wistaria trailing its lovely French grey blossoms over trellis and wall; Bougainvillia with its many-shaded, yellow-centred bloom, that always stirs one's heart with suggestions of the East; the "Gloria pea" (a sort of majestic fuchsia growing in large bushes here); and a number of New Zealand flowering shrubs,—all beautiful in form and colour, but many of them strangers to me in those days, before I had set foot in that far-away and yet most home-like colony.

After the "eternal gum-tree," one of the most common and characteristic of the Tasmanian trees is the silver wattle. It has feathery dark green leaves, and lovely yellow fluffy blossoms like tiny balls. Beautiful heathers line the roads all over the island, and were now in full bloom in every shade of cream, white, salmon, and crimson; such heathers as we at home keep in our greenhouses in tiny pots, and cherish with most tender care.

Every one visiting Hobart goes to New Norfolk, on the beautiful Derwent River, either by boat or steamer, or by train and coach. We chose the latter route. The railway runs below the Botanical Gardens, and then along the line of the river, giving one every chance of seeing the scenery, for Tasmanian trains are very slow. The views here are not so much grand as lovely and peaceful, reminding one often of the nooks and exquisite reaches of our own Thames.

On leaving the train, a beautiful ten-mile drive over a heather-lined road, through woods of silver wattle and eucalyptus, deposited us at the "Star and Garter," a quiet little inn in the pretty township of New Norfolk. After early dinner, we climbed a hill to get a view over the river towards the snow-clad peaks of Mount Field, in the far distance, and, scrambling down on the other side, passed a pretty little stone Roman Catholic church, just built and not yet consecrated. Close by was a cosy, low stone house, whose owner was taking a quiet siesta in his veranda. He told us a good deal about the fisheries, and the late experiments to introduce salmon into Tasmania. Seven miles from New Norfolk are the salmon-ponds where the attempt has been made, but so far with little success.

The salmon either get away down to the sea, or so completely change their nature in these waters as to be no longer recognizable as salmon, becoming quite coarse and uneatable. Attempts to supplement Nature out here do not seem successful on the whole, or else the Acclimatization Society have been singularly unfortunate in their choice. Sparrows are not indigenous to the soil, and the kind

brought over here have certainly grown and thriven, but
have become scourges instead of scavengers.

It is the same with the rabbits—that prolific curse of
the colonies! It seems to be a very dangerous experiment
either to introduce a new species of animal into a colony
or to exterminate an old one.

In either case, it is impossible to discount beforehand all
the dangers and drawbacks that may follow such a course
until it has been taken and the mischief is irremediable.
This appears to me the weak point in Pasteur's scheme of
poison. Isolated experiments can never be conclusive. The
fact that certain animals or insects on certain occasions have
abstained from taking the poison is no absolute proof that
all useful animals and insects will continue to do so upon
all occasions, when the field of experiment is measured by
thousands of acres—not a small inclosure of ground specially
set apart for the purpose.

Moreover, even in these scientific days, there may be
insects and birds doing useful and invaluable work in the
world of Nature that we know not of, and shall only
appreciate properly when some ill-considered experiment of
ours may have exterminated them from the field of their
labour.

Talking of birds reminds me of my childish feeling of
pleasure and amazement in seeing parroquets and cocka-
toos flying from tree to tree, flashing their gorgeous colours
in the sunshine, in this beautiful island.

All birds have brilliant colouring here. The magpies are much larger than ours, looking more like huge crows with white wings. The robins have such deep flame-coloured breasts, putting their poor little English brothers quite in the shade. The "fire-tail," a sober-coloured dark little bird with exquisite crimson feathers in the tail alone, is common enough here, but strikes one with an ever-growing sense of delight, as he flashes from tree to tree with his little fire-signal at his back.

One of the more ambitious and most beautiful expeditions from Hobart is to go up the Huon River by steamer, returning next day by coach. As this involves sleeping out, few people care to do it, but it will well repay the small exertion, and is by no means an expensive expedition as colonial prices go.

We left Hobart at 8.30 A.M. on board the *Cygnet*, one of several small steamers which ply between that town and the various landing-stages along the Huon.

After taking in all the beauties of the harbour, which we had missed upon the night of our arrival, I could turn my attention to more prosaic matters, and accepted the engineer's invitation to go down to the engine-rooms and watch an experiment for burning anthracite coal at twelve shillings the ton and a product of Tasmania, instead of paying twenty-four shillings for bituminous Sydney coal. My *cicerone* said that the firemen were unjustly prejudiced against the use of the native coal. No doubt the latter gives extra work, and the heat thrown out by it seemed small out of all comparison

with the amount given out by the more expensive article;
in which case I should doubt the final economy of the
experiment, even allowing for the saving of 50 per cent.
on the original outlay.

The Hobart climate in October (spring) seems quite as
variable as our own. Sunshine and shadow succeed each
other as quickly as in our English April, and the month
here certainly deserves its name of " chill October." Last
year, I am told that when the first stone of the new deanery
was laid, at exactly the same season, the heat was intense and
almost unbearable.

Be that as it may, we had a very cold trip through
D'Entrecasteaux Channel to the mouth of the river, and
thence to Franklin, a pretty township, situated on the hills
and surrounded by lovely mountains. Here we had arranged
to sleep, and take the coach next day for the return journey.

The chief inn (a very primitive one) was redolent of paint,
and evidently in the hands of workmen, so we put up at a
small temperance hotel, and my only experience of such an
establishment was really a very comfortable one. Our host
and hostess, young married people, sat down with us at tea and
at breakfast next day, as also a young man living with them,
who was police clerk to the district. The latter gave us an
amusing account of a fellow passenger in our steamer. She
had come on board at the first stopping-place after Hobart,
and we had been attracted by the very gay, fantastically
trimmed Tam-o'-Shanter straw hat which she wore. Later

on, after leaving Shipwright's Point, she had the boat of
the steamer lowered, jumped into it, and began sculling
herself across to the other side (a very considerable distance),
and in the teeth of a very strong current. The captain told
us she had done this every day of her life for twelve years
past, carrying the post and any parcels that might arrive for
the little homestead where she lives. The uncle and aunt, in
whose house she abides, own one of the largest orchards in
Tasmania, and must be people of substance. This enterprising young woman seems to be a " Jack (or Jill) of all
trades." In addition to the more domestic accomplishments
of cookery and dairy tending, she can carpenter, sow, reap,
plough, and " do as much work out of doors in one day as
any two men." Moreover, she will ride, drive, or row twenty
or thirty miles to a ball at any time ; dance all night, and
return in the same way next morning. Certainly, she
looked very much weather-beaten, but is said to have been
rather good-looking in younger days, before this mania for
hard work came on.

Next morning we rose early, and were out by 7 A.M. for
a stroll amongst the beautiful hills, and were quite sorry
to leave the pretty little primitive village when the coach
came round for us at 9 A.M.

We drove through the pretty township of Victoria, which
is more shut in than Franklin, and must be hotter and less
healthy as a summer resort, I imagine. Then we followed
the river's side for some miles, until gradually the very

excellent road began to ascend, and by degrees we reached a considerable elevation. Here we passed the prettiest part of the road, where the tree fern grows in great profusion, and to an immense height.

Our host, Mr. Webster, turned out to be also our Jehu, and wonderfully well he drove, being one of several brothers of the same name who "boss" this coach line on the Huon road, and have houses of similar harmless entertainment along the whole extent of it. The road, which measures twenty-three miles from Victoria to Hobart, was made by Government at an outlay of £28,000.

After lunch, we drove on to a gradual elevation of 1,500 feet, getting every now and then beautiful peeps of the bay and the surrounding mountains. Then began the descent into the town, and by 3 P.M. we were once more at Hobart Post Office, where the coach stops to discharge prisoners. These coaches are very primitive machines, with black leather curtains which cover either side, but which can be reefed or let down at pleasure. Inside the coach, however, it is impossible to get any good view, and it is therefore most necessary to insure the box seat beforehand.

If any one, having one whole day to spend in this lovely island, asked me how to make the best use of the time, I should advise a morning drive to the Cornelian Bay Cemetery, by the side of the Derwent, and commanding a magnificent view of the river, bay, and surrounding mountains.

For the afternoon, I should recommend a drive of ten miles, partly along the Huon road, already mentioned, to a place on the sea-shore, called Brown's River, from the stream that winds through a rocky ravine, and empties itself into the sea at this point, and where the most exquisite shells of every size, hue, and shape, can be picked up on the shore, even by the most lazy conchologist.

I had made friends with an intelligent jeweller in Hobart, to whom I had taken a ring that required some small repair, and as he has travelled all over the Australasian colonies before anchoring for a time in Hobart, his conversation and experiences were well worth hearing.

Having gathered from some casual words that he was convinced of the truths of spiritualism (as it is called), I was somewhat surprised when he handed me a thick book full of newspaper "cuttings," describing the "excellent lectures given by Lieutenant Rose (the man in question) to expose spiritualism."

It seemed a paradox that a man, himself a spiritualist, should spend his life in giving lectures to expose his own beliefs.

He admitted the force of my remark, but said quietly that *it would never pay* to lecture in favour of the creed. There was so much prejudice against the subject, that, on one occasion, when through some misunderstanding he was announced as an advocate of it, the scene of confusion was terrible. The whole lecture-hall was converted into a bear-garden, oranges, rotten eggs, and even chairs, flying gaily around; and it was not until the audience was assured that Mr. Ross intended to "curse" instead of to "bless," so far as their *bête noir* was concerned, that they consented to give him any sort of a hearing.

"I was not likely to lecture in favour of spiritualism after that sort of thing," he said, very frankly.

My denunciation of the dishonesty of his present practice seemed to fall like water off a duck's back.

"Yes, of course, I know from experience that it is true enough," he said; "but I am bound to make a living, and they won't listen to anything else. Besides, there *is* a good deal of trickery and fraud amongst some of the professional mediums, so it is fair enough to expose *them*."

He seemed unable to see the dishonesty of leaving his audience to infer that he believed there was nothing *but* trickery and deception in the matter.

I wonder how much more of the "exposure of spiritualism" may be done on similar lines?

To turn to more orthodox matters, I went to the Cathedral one Sunday morning, and heard a clever but rather intrepid sermon from Bishop Sandford on the words "*One Lord.*"

He attacked the subject of the miracles, and showed an ingenuity in dealing with them which is a necessary clerical attribute in these days of universal scepticism on all matters, mundane or divine.

He tried to prove that the miracles were no *reversing* of the order of Nature, but rather, as it were, pushing Nature back from what was unnatural into the natural groove again. For example, in the miracle of raising the dead, "life is the law of Nature, therefore Christ only restored the natural law in raising Lazarus from the dead."

This struck me as more ingenious than fair, for surely death is equally a law of Nature as we know her, and we cannot logically go beyond human experience in speaking of natural laws ?

Nothing daunted, the Bishop next attacked the miracle of turning water into wine at the marriage feast in Cana of Galilee :—

"This was no new process—only a recognized process performed instantly instead of through long weeks and months. Water is being turned into wine every day. The water nourishes the roots of the vine, making the grapes grow, and from them is expressed the wine we drink."

Or, again, with regard to the miracle of feeding the five thousand with the five small loaves :—

"We cast grain into the ground, and God gives the increase which we gather at the harvest. The process was only *accelerated* when the loaves were miraculously increased to meet the wants of the multitude."

This seems terribly far-fetched, and is a fair specimen of the specious clerical arguments of a really manly and honest mind, compelled by the spirit of the age to find an excuse or explanation for what had surely better be left to the domain of faith.

I felt much more sympathy with him at the end of the discourse, when he spoke very humbly and beautifully of the difficulties of the problems of life to all thinking minds.

"The scientific men call upon us to choose between power and love in our Creator. If He is omnipotent, He is cruel: if He is love, He is not omnipotent."

As we are not able with our present powers to grasp even the whole meaning of *Nature*, surely we cannot expect by their aid to understand and search out the inscrutable wisdom of the Creator.

Therefore it is not illogical to say, "We will *believe* in His love *and* omnipotence in spite of appearances."

There was a straightforward manliness in the way he faced and disposed of the difficulty at the last that came like a breath of strong, wholesome fresh air after the artificial atmosphere of subtle theological suggestion.

One of the chief personal interests in my visit to Tasmania lay in the fact that we are here surrounded by recollections of the governorship of Sir John Franklin, whose grandchildren are amongst my valued friends.

There is a very fine bronze statue of Sir John in the public square in Hobart, called after his name. The long, low house where he lived (before the present grand new

residence existed) was pointed out to me by the Dean,
and is situated almost opposite the present deanery. A
whole village on the Huon River has been called after
the famous explorer; and the setting sun of my Tasmanian
experiences lights up the face of this great man, whose
name shines forth through the ever-lengthening years with
as bright a memory and as keen a sadness as in the days
when hope deferred at last died out a lingering death,
and men knew that they should see his face no more
"until the Sea gives up her dead."

CHAPTER II.

SYDNEY AND MELBOURNE.

HAVING waited patiently for nearly a month in Tasmania, in the vain hope that the small-pox scare might subside and the quarantine regulations be at least suspended, I hardened my heart at length, and took ship for Sydney in the Tas-

manian Steam Navigation boat *Flora*, determined to risk
the chance of quarantine sooner than spend the rest of my
natural life in Hobart Town, as there seemed to be every
chance of my doing.

As no steamers that had touched the Tasmanian coast were
allowed to enter either Australian or New Zealand ports,
postal communication was deficient, if not impossible; and,
moreover, I had not received a line from the friend I had
come so far to join, and felt naturally anxious to know where
the meeting could be effected.

My last letters from her had come from Sydney, where
I pictured her awaiting my arrival. It turned out that,
weary of the delay, she had gone off to New Zealand, but
I had no idea of this fact at the time, or might possibly
never have seen the Australian Colonies at all.

As it was, we came in for one of the most tremendous
gales that had visited even the stormy Australian coast
for many years.

A well-known steamer, *The Cheviot*, of the Howard Smith
line, went down in the storm at 9 P.M. on the night after
we left Hobart, with a loss of thirty-seven passengers out
of sixty on board, and most of the officers and crew.
The wreck occurred just outside Melbourne Heads.

The stern of the vessel was lifted by the storm so violently out of the water, that the "racing" of the propeller
ended by snapping it off, and the vessel drifted on to the
rocks, where she was cleft completely in two parts.

Her bows struck the rocks first, and all the steerage passengers were lost. The saloon passengers and the captain were saved.

The latter behaved splendidly after the disaster had occurred, but was considered foolhardy for putting out to sea on such a night.

In the court of inquiry that was afterwards held, special mention was made of the fact that various other vessels advertised to sail that evening had not left the harbour—notably one of the Union Steam Navigation boats, the *Wairarapa*.

The counsel for the captain quietly explained this away by saying, " *That* ship had some very valuable animals on board," which must have provoked a smile even on that solemn occasion.

The explanation, however, is more reasonable and less cynical than would appear at first sight.

We must remember that valuable cattle, being stowed on the lower deck, might easily be washed overboard in a sea not heavy enough to endanger the ship herself or the lives of the passengers or crew.

Our own captain's boldness was justified by success, and the *Flora* reached Sydney Harbour in safety on the evening of Thursday, October 20th, forty-eight hours out from Hobart, having made one of the quickest passages on record, but earned the undying hatred of most of us who sailed in her, for one naturally identifies a ship with the amount of misery suffered whilst on board her.

D

We steamed into Sydney Harbour and cast anchor in Watson's Bay between **7** P.M. and 8 P.M., too late for the daylight; but one scarcely regretted it, for a full moon and a starlit sky lent a beautiful and more poetic setting to the scene, and the numerous coloured lights from the masses of rigging on all sides gave a fairy-like look to the famous harbour.

This harbour (from later experience) strikes me as more *home-like*, in spite of its great expanse, than any similar scenery on such a grand scale.

Quebec, for example (magnificent as is the harbour view), seems much less "friendly" as our German neighbours would say—a panorama to be gazed at with admiration, whereas you take Sydney Harbour straight into your heart and love it for once and for ever.

The low-lying hills around, the numerous small bays, the lovely green islands dotted all over the broad bosom of the harbour, form a truly magnificent sight; and yet you can take it in without effort, and feel as though you could quickly grow familiar with all the beautiful bends and turns of the sea.

This, I think, must be the secret of the almost passionate devotion of all Australians for this favoured spot.

Other harbours may be as lovely, some few may be as grand, but it would be difficult to name *one* that combines the magnificent and the lovable in any like proportion.

Of course the overwhelming admiration from the practical and naval point of view arises from the fact that no other harbour in the world has such depth of water and can boast of such easy navigation.

Even Melbourne does full justice to Sydney on this score, and reluctantly admits that *she* has nothing to compare with the world-famed " harbour."

" But this is an accident of nature," adds the jealous sister colony. " Look what we have made out of our possibilities compared with the provincial, dead-alive look of the capital of New South Wales."

Small wonder that " the harbour " should be the boast, the pride, and the joy of every man, woman, and child in Sydney. The possibilities of enjoyment connected with it are countless. From the " Circular Quay " you can take steamers for trips in every direction, spend an hour or two rambling through some lovely wooded dell, or walking over a road that commands grand views of wood and sea, and so gain some further spot from which another steamer will bring you back to the hot dusty city.

There is not a beautiful spot in all this vast stretch of beauty that cannot be reached by steamer in times varying from ten to sixty minutes, whilst excursions to the heads and all round the harbour are of frequent occurrence, and occupy some two or three hours of a delicious summer's day or still more romantic moonlight night.

It requires some experience of the stifling, enervating heat of a Sydney spring or summer in order to appreciate fully the enormous relief of one of these harbour trips, with its cool soft breezes, in exchange for the hot dusty pavements of the hilly Sydney streets.

I am loth to leave the beauty and charm of Sydney Harbour, feeling there is so little else about the place that I can honestly admire. But after all, Sydney *is* Sydney Harbour. All the fashionable suburbs of the town are built upon its shores, and the dirty, dusty old town itself need rarely be visited by the happy possessors of the many charming houses that lie in every direction upon the surrounding hills.

The town of Sydney is much scattered, and built upon numerous hills. One is always going full pelt down one steep hill only to find an equally steep one to be mounted on the other side. The dust when I was there was perfectly appalling, and as a hot north-east wind blew continually, the charms of the Australian climate did not strike me at once with any great force, and I thought the *World* had spoken with little charity and less knowledge in reproaching Mrs. Barry so bitterly for finding any flaw in Sydney weather. In spring, I know from experience that the Sydney climate is extremely trying to a new-comer. The heat during the summer months is of course intense, and during the winter there are often weeks of continuous rain. Naturally, you are told that the weather is "most exceptional" at such times; but I found, after several months' experience, that colonial weather was invariably "exceptional" when it was not perfect. Writing under the fog-bound misery of a London

January, one would hail even Sydney heat and dust with delight, but it is as well to realize that cloudless skies and brilliant sunshine must be paid for like everything else in this world—at least in Australia.

The Botanical Gardens which run down to the water, and occupy a considerable line along the harbour, are most extensive and beautiful, but not very well kept as a whole. It was amusing to notice how much more care was bestowed upon those parts of the grounds which surrounded Government House, built at the top of the gardens, overlooking the harbour.

Spring is scarcely the best time to see tropical gardens. Many of the shrubs and plants are dried up by the early heat, whilst others, more prudent, have not yet attempted to bud. One of the chief trees about here is the Queensland fig, a large spreading tree, with stiff green leaves in clusters, and little hard brown balls, which develop into small red-coloured figs, rounder and smaller than our green fig.

The pleasantest fruit I have tasted out here is the *loquart*. It is a small, round, yellow, and slightly acid fruit, and grows in clusters with long narrow green leaves to the stems.

The passion fruit which is so universally appreciated is far too luscious for my taste, and I grew to dislike even the perfume of it.

I came across a celebrated *pianiste* in Sydney—a young French lady married to a German-Australian. She gives music-lessons, has a large *clientèle* amongst the Sydney "upper ten," and has a novel and excellent method of teaching.

She forms a class of five pupils, and divides an hour and forty minutes amongst them. Each girl appropriates twenty minutes of this time, and each plays the same study or the same movement, whilst the other four listen and profit by the mistakes and instruction of their friends.

The plan seems to answer admirably, judging by the lady's success, and as she manages to find time also to bring up three little children (all under two and a half years of age), she must have immense energy, and more physical strength than one can well imagine with so small a frame.

She played to me, on several occasions, selections from Beethoven, Gottschalk, Chopin, &c., with equally brilliant and unerring touch, and, apart from the charm of the music, it was quite a pretty sight to see the tiny hands flashing over the piano.

Marvelling at the many prizes won so early in life by Mr. Bertram Wise, late Attorney-General for New South Wales, I was assured that all successful barristers out here are making from £1,500 to £3,000 or £4,000 a year, and then retire on judgeships varying from £3,000 to £7,000 a year. This, of course, means good luck as well as brains. Still, I wonder that some of our *capable* English barristers, who think themselves lucky if they clear £1,500 a year by the time they are forty, do not come out here and tempt Fortune on a bigger scale.

Mechanical headwork is useless, but real talent must find a wider field where the competition is less fierce than in our overcrowded island.

Mrs. Wise being an old friend of mine in England, I had many pleasant and sociable evenings with her and her clever young husband in their pretty home "on" Macleay Street, the fashionable Sydney street of many handsome residences, and somewhat reminding me of our Palace Gardens.

In company with Mr. and Mrs. Wise I made my first and last appearance in the Sydney House of Parliament. It is at present a most unpretentious, mean-looking, long, low house in Macquarie Street, as little remarkable inside as it is from the outside. A Speaker's chair, a few leather stuffed seats on either side, for the Government and the Opposition respectively, and a gallery at the end, pretty well crowded with spectators (who, I trust, were edified by what they saw and heard), completed the *entourage*.

Who was the great statesman who remarked, " With how little wisdom the world is governed ! " ? How often that sentence flashed through my brain as I sat in the Sydney House for three mortal hours listening to the most undignified " wrangle " from the Opposition, which continually fell to the level of personality and abuse, and threatened to sink to the still lower depths of a free fight.

It seemed that the previous evening some member of the Government had stigmatized the conduct of some members of the Opposition as " contemptible and notorious "—on the

vexed question of obstruction. The expressions had been used
and withdrawn twenty-four hours previously, but the war raged
on with a flow of invective as dull as it was disgraceful.

One of the Opposition, an undertaker, was specially
violent, and had a depressed and vicious expression, as
though he had lived amongst corpses all his life, and had
not been improved by his surroundings.

The members of the Government certainly showed to
great advantage on this occasion, as they sat in almost
unbroken silence listening to the flood of abuse and
personalities that surged around them from the Opposition
benches. "A set of dirty tools" was one of the mildest
terms of reproach hurled at them; but possibly they would
have been less forbearing and perhaps less dignified had the
respective positions been reversed.

One fears that such lamentable want of good taste and
good breeding can scarcely be confined to either side of the
House. The abuse, moreover, was so utterly stupid. They
never seemed able to see an opening for a good point by
which the adversary's weapons might have been turned
inwards. One was reminded of those lines—

> " Satire is like a penknife, sharp and keen,
> Which while it penetrates is scarcely seen ;
> But thine, the oyster knife that hacks and hews—
> The will, but not the power, to abuse."

To me the whole proceedings appeared an undignified,
childlike, ill-bred, dishonest waste of the time that should

have been spent in the real interests of the country, and can only serve as a terrible warning to our own House of Commons, should the days ever come when mass shall outweigh merit.

The poor Speaker rose several times with calls "to order," and seemed both annoyed and disgusted, but helpless to administer more than a temporary extinguisher, after which the "honourable member" flew up again, more rampant than ever. At five o'clock we came out to a pleasant diversion in the form of tea in the Committee-room, where the Leader of the Opposition, the Sergeant-at-Arms, and several other members were introduced to me. The Leader of the Opposition (Mr. Dibbs) told me that on more than one occasion he had been present at a sitting of fifty-six hours—once from Thursday till Sunday afternoon. Beds and blankets were brought into the Committee-rooms, and the members were literally "packed," to be awakened whenever a division took place. One man spoke for nine hours consecutively, in order to gain time, and managed, it is said, to cling to some coherence in spite of his lengthy speech. All this was told with great triumph, but sounds rather derogatory to the dignity of the House, when we consider that it sprang from a mere party trick to starve and weary out the other side through sheer physical exhaustion—surely not a very noble way of getting the best of an argument.

The Government represents the Free Trade policy, and

I was glad to have the opportunity of hearing Sir Henry Parkes speak after tea. He is a striking-looking old man, with a thick shock of pure white hair, and a face something between that of a lion and a bulldog. He has a very low sweet voice, that can, however, ring out with great strength when he is repelling a charge or protesting against an injustice. His language is remarkably well chosen, and the words fall naturally and without effort into their appropriate places, so much so as to give a sense of rest and completeness that not even the absence of every legitimate *h*, and the introduction of a good many extraneous ones, can disturb. I can quite understand his power in reading men, and the magnetic influence he exercises over those who come nearest to him. He is always appealing to the *feelings* of his audience; there is a sort of perpetual *Julius Cæsar* and *Mark Antony* flavour in his speeches; whilst any suspicion of weakness or sentimentality is kept in check by flashes of the old Roman senator passion, which are judiciously introduced from time to time.

One has a chronic feeling that he is a most noble, long-suffering, much-enduring, and slightly unappreciated patriot. I suppose this is because he is perpetually conveying such an impression to every one.

Anyway, his quiet voice and well-chosen words came as a great relief after the unmannerly, vulgar, and bearish behaviour of many of the members.

The Attorney-General took but little part in the debate

on this occasion beyond asking a few questions; his bright refined face and quiet gentlemanly bearing seemed singularly out of place with his surroundings.

It is not to be wondered at that so few respectable men out here can be found to take part in politics with this contaminating atmosphere.

Motives of purest patriotism must be required to induce any honourable man to mix himself up with such company, at the risk of suffering possibly for life from their foul lies and insinuations against his private character.

Yet, unless more such men can be found, it is hard to see whence political salvation is to come. The outlook is a dreary one at present : boxing-gloves bid fair to take the place of truth and reason in the arguments of the future.

In the company of kind friends I made all the pleasanter expeditions in the vicinity of Sydney. We had a picnic to Middle Harbour, which takes the cake for beauty as the colonists would say. We drove to the South Head Lighthouse, devoted a long summer afternoon away upon Manley Beach, explored the lovely Lane Cove River, and spent one melting, never-to-be-forgotten day in Paramatta, which town boasts of a fine collegiate school (King's), but is chiefly interesting as having been the site of the former residence of the Governor. Old Government House still remains as a memory of the past, in the Paramatta Park.

Going to Paramatta by steamer from Sydney, one passes

numerous specimens of the mangrove, a tree which grows in the water, and serves to reclaim the land by pushing forward its roots, and so by degrees presenting an impenetrable barrier to the encroaching waters. The branches of these trees are thick and stumpy, especially towards the roots, and the foliage is very dense, not unlike the Queensland fig-tree at first sight.

Of course I "did" my Blue Mountains like the rest of the world, but this scenery has been so fully described that it is unnecessary to dwell upon it. My week in the mountain district was a rainy one, with a few bright exceptions, when the beautiful scenery seemed all the more beautiful for emerging from such a mist of tears. To be able to reach this glorious scenery and bracing climate within four hours by train from Sydney, must be a matter for devout thankfulness to every one living near the metropolis.

I stayed at Katoomba, a very central point, from which all expeditions can be made.

My first day, being doubtful as regards weather, was devoted to investigating the rail beyond Katoomba, and specially the famous "zig-zag"—a loop-line which is a modified edition of the one near Georgetown in the Rocky Mountains. The train rises by a very heavy grade to a point overlooking some deep cliffs; here the engine reverses and runs down a graduated incline, looping backwards and forwards until the zig-zag platform is finally reached on the plains beneath. A great deal of coal is found in these mountains, and we saw many of the pits' mouths from the train, and also in walking from Eskbank to the dirty coal-mining town of Littigon.

Silver has lately been discovered in great quantities about eight miles beyond Littigon, and I met a man on this expedition who seemed much excited by the mining prospects recently opened out.

He "hailed" from Sydenham, England, but had spent thirty years in the colonies, and spoke with great horror of the rough bush life. "Ease of manner," according to his account, seems to degenerate into very decided license of speech and conduct, and the utter absence of the most ordinary decencies of life. Govett's Leap is the expedition *par excellence* in the Blue Mountains, but I thought Wentworth Falls quite as beautiful, and the features of the scenery are curiously similar in all these mountain expeditions. The same grand panorama meets your eye everywhere. Miles upon miles of thick "scrub" in the valley below, sharp precipitous rocks rising around you in the form of a vast amphitheatre, whilst you look sheer down—down into the unfathomable depths of the virgin forest, and almost shudder to feel suspended, as it were, in mid air over such a weird mysterious scene. The waterfall, as usual, is merely an accident, breaking the curve of the natural amphitheatre very pleasantly, and forming a damp bed for the exquisite ferns which grow up its rocky sides. I clambered down to various points, or "look-outs," guarded by iron railings, built over the giddy heights. The glorious line of blue mountains (so well deserving their name), stretched out for miles into the far horizon, dying away at length into the sky-line, from which it was so hard to distinguish them. The scenery here is above all *characteristic*, quite unlike any other I have seen; and just now (November), the monotony of green foliage was constantly broken up by clumps of *waratah*, a glorious mountain flower which only blossoms at this time of the year. In shape it is somewhat like a glorified globe artichoke, but of deepest crimson, and grows on stalks as thick as one's finger some two or three feet from the ground, springing up from the dark green leaves which wave around the gorgeous blossoms. Many beautiful specimens of *Erica* (specially the *white* heather) abound in this mountainous district, which is also a very paradise of ferns. The comfortable Katoomba Hotel had a very judicial flavour at the time of my visit, reckoning no less than three judges with their wives, and in one case a family, amongst its guests.

Sir William Stawell, formerly one of the most famous judges in Victoria, but whose health, alas! has broken down under the strain of work, was amongst these. I had much talk over colonial matters with Lady Stawell, who spoke very highly of the energy and education of "the people." Her remarks referred, of course, to Victoria, not to New South Wales, and there appears a vast difference between the two countries, which are yet so nearly allied by situation and climate. To begin with, New South Wales must have much

more of the old convict blood in its veins. Melbourne is
a newer city, and has been colonized from a very different
class in England, who went out to carve their fortunes by
industry and energy, and were not generally sent "for the
good of their country." Even those who came to Victoria
on compulsion did so generally for trifling offences. Minor
criminals were transported frequently, not because their
crimes were specially heinous, but as a matter of expediency
to colonize a country which seemed so far off thirty or forty
years ago that bribes of money or land were found useless
in urging men to undertake what was then a very lengthy
and perilous voyage.

New South Wales, on the contrary, had been started in
the older days, when convicts *were* convicts, and the first
idea was to provide a safe place for them, and not to extend
a rising colony. Much of my talk with Lady Stawell was
on the vexed question of domestic service out here. She
and many other mistresses have told me that Australian
servants are on an absolutely different footing from those
in England, but it would appear in some ways a more
wholesome and pleasant one. It seems that you must
readjust your views of domestic service here entirely, or you
will get nothing done for you at all. "Treat a Colonial
servant as you would an English one, and see where you pull
up." Lady Stawell was guiltless of the Yankee expression,
but that seemed the text of her discourse. You must look
upon servants here as obliging sort of people who live in

your house and are willing to work if you treat them very
well and consider it a matter of mutual accommodation.
They require more individuality of life, and exact time for
reading, working, and holidays, in a way that would
scare an English mistress. Give in to this with a good
grace, and I am assured that you can often secure faithful
and devoted service. Three ladies present on this occasion
spoke of servants who had lived with them for eight, ten,
and twelve years respectively, showing real unselfish devotion
in times of sickness and trouble. We English seem to fall
between two stools in this matter, and servants have come to
look upon us as natural enemies, or as weak fools if we
attempt to rule by kindness. The old feudal system between
master and servant, still surviving in parts of France, seems
to answer very well, as also the advanced Colonial idea of
equality of rights and citizenship. We seem to be in the
transition stage between the two, and the result is as
uncomfortable as incongruous positions invariably must be.

On my return to Sydney from the Blue Mountains, I
spent two very pleasant days on the Woodstock estate, near
Rooty Hill, a station on the line, some twenty miles from
Sydney, and the country residence of Mr. Walter Lamb.

My host, who has also a charming house in Sydney, is
a well-known breeder of stock, but has lately given fresh
impetus to local industry on his estate by starting a fruit-
canning establishment on his own grounds. He has let a
large portion of the Woodstock estate to small holders, on

the understanding that the land should be devoted to fruit-growing, and has raised a substantial brick structure, seventy-four feet in length by thirty-one in height, for receiving, cutting up, and canning the fruit. All the tins are manufactured on the premises, where every operation connected with the industry takes place. The great difficulty, the water supply, has been met by constructing an extensive reservoir, capable of holding 3,000,000 gallons of water, whilst a circular cemented brick tank with a capacity of 22,000 gallons has been constructed in front of the building, and is worked by a wind-mill from the main reservoir. The land is admirably suited for orchard purposes, being composed of gently rolling hills and undulating slopes, offering grand facilities for water storage. As the works develop, still larger reservoirs will be built, and steam power used to pump the water into tanks distributed over the locality. More than a hundred acres of land (to be increased to a thousand) have been already planted with peaches, apricots, pears, plums, and quinces, but fruit is also received at remunerative prices from many outside sources. Mr. Lamb has travelled all over California to acquaint himself with the newest machinery and the various processes for preserving fruit on a large scale, and his aim is to develop this industry in New South Wales, and enable her to compete with California as one of the great fruit markets of the world.

Australia moreover starts with one striking advantage.

E

California has to buy all the sugar used for syrup-making, whereas New South Wales can raise it on her own ground. Mr. Lamb spoke most enthusiastically of the generous kindness he had universally met with from the great "fruit canners" of California when they heard the object of his visit. Far from showing any petty jealousy in the matter they vied with each other in affording him every facility for seeing the details of the working of their various establishments.

One of my last evenings in Sydney was devoted to the Criterion Theatre, in order that I might see the great Australian theatrical star, Miss Essie Jenyns, who was playing Viola in *Twelfth Night*. I had heard such exaggerated accounts of her beauty and genius that it was perhaps natural to find the reality far below my expectations. It is almost unfair to criticize so young an actress severely; but Australians claim for her a place far above Ellen Terry, which is absurd. She is a pretty, intelligent girl, has been well and carefully taught, and does great credit to her teachers, making the most of the powers Nature has bestowed upon her. But she has not to my mind the most crude possibilities for anything like a great actress. There was no flash of inspiration, no one great moment throughout, nor do I think that she ever forgot that she was Miss Essie Jenyns, a very charming girl, deeply beloved and vainly adored by all the youth of Sydney.[1]

I must not leave Sydney without mention of a very inter-

[1] I have recently heard of the marriage of this popular young lady to a gentleman of good position and large fortune in Sydney.

esting afternoon spent with Professor Threlfall, who fills the Chair of Natural Philosophy at Sydney University, and kindly volunteered to show me his laboratory and something of the University buildings, which are very extensive. The magnificent hall used for "Commemoration," and built in the Elizabethan style, is the most striking of these. The painted windows are very fine specimens of artistic colour and taste. There is a fine carved wooden roof supported by angels, and a very grand organ, divided into three parts, with the warm colouring of a painted window serving as a background for it.

The new medical schools are being built on a very fine scale, and Professor Threlfall is himself planning and super-intending the building of a new laboratory, a plain work-manlike structure but fitted up with every convenience.

He complained of the difficulty of keeping within the limits of a grant of £13,000, which seems a fair sum for the purpose, but labour commands very high prices in these parts.

My remembrance of a visit to the Art Museum in Sydney is almost too melancholy to be recalled. The building re-minds one irresistibly of a red brick stable, and speaks more for the absence of feeling for art in the Colonies than a hundred articles written upon the subject could do. The collection of sculpture is very poor. Some war pieces by De Neuville, and a few originals of well-known works by Millais and Leighton, represent the pictures, but there is

little evidence of local talent with the exception of one or
two Tasmanian views and one of the Goulburn River. There
are some good engravings, but these are all by English or
European artists, and there is without doubt a wide opening,
to be filled in the future, let us hope, by talent native to
the soil.

Having a lively remembrance of my sufferings on board
the *Flora*, I determined to go overland from Sydney to
Melbourne, some eighteen hours by train, with one or two
changes *en route*. America might take one lesson from
Australia, viz. in the arrangements of the Pulman cars at
night. A shifting door divides the ladies from the gentlemen, the position of the door in the car being regulated
by the numbers of berths engaged for either sex : married
couples are separated, of course, by this arrangement, but if
" the greater happiness of the greater number " is to be
considered, there is no question of the advantages of this
system over the crude American method.

Melbourne claims to remind one of America more than
any other Colonial city. So it does, and the boast is not
peculiarly vainglorious, for it would be hard to find anything in ugliness to beat the usual type of American city,
Boston and Washington always excepted.

Melbourne, however, possesses some really fine buildings,
and the Botanical Gardens are even more beautiful here
than in Sydney, although the latter can boast the finer
situation of the two, thanks to the immortal harbour. Mel-

bourne has certainly gone ahead of Sydney with regard to
the Houses of Parliament, which are very handsome. The
original building is thirty years old—quite historical out
here; but within the last ten years some fine rooms have
been added, and two new wings are being built, which will
make an imposing finish to the structure. A beautiful little
cupola rises in the middle of the buildings, and the gilding
and ornamentation are in very good taste.

A distinguished member took me all over the Houses, and
told me, with great pride, that the size of the table and the
distance between the Speaker and the seats are the same as
in London. In one of the rooms I saw the original green
leather-covered Speaker's chair used in the English House
of Commons, from 1835 to 1853, and presented by Viscount
Canterbury, when out here, in remembrance of his father,
Lord John Manners.

The Speaker in the Victoria House wears a wig, and
therefore looks more imposing than his official brother of
New South Wales. Let us hope he also commands a little
more respect.

It is said that, so far as manners go, there is not much to
choose between the two Houses; but upon this occasion the
Melbourne debate was at least respectable, if somewhat dull.
All the members spoke at once, and seemed anxious to drown
each other's voices; but one learns to be thankful for small
mercies, and the absence of violent personal abuse was very
grateful, and full of blissful repose. I believe that here, as

elsewhere, atmosphere must have some influence. Possibly, a shabby old "House" may have as demoralizing an effect on some masses of men as a shabby old coat has been known to have upon many an individual.

My kind *cicerone* gave me an exhaustive, but rather complicated, idea of Victoria politics. The two parties here seem to have divided simply upon the question of taxation. The plutocracy of course wish for an easy scale, and the extreme Radicals insist upon severe taxation and a "sliding" scale, so that a man with a thousand acres should pay less upon each acre than the proud possessor of two thousand would do. Between these two extremes comes the Moderate Liberal party, who approve of taxing real estate but disapprove of the sliding scale, and are in favour of an equal tax on land, apart from any question as to the extent of the "holding."

The Public Library is a very fine building in the Grecian style, well supplied with books, which are free to all who come to read. I was delighted to see so many men availing themselves of such a privilege, but rather disappointed to find that most of them were reading novels at 11.30 A.M., very few scientific or literary books being in request on the morning of my visit.

The Melbourne Picture Gallery is on a far finer scale than the Sydney "Art (stable)," and a loan exhibition of pictures from London, called the "Grosvenor Gallery," was going on when I paid my visit there. In the Parliament Gallery it was interesting to witness the hanging of Orchardson's "First Cloud," and a fine sea piece by Peter Graham, which had only that morning arrived from England.

There is one most delightful arrangement which obtains in these Colonies, but men as usual have the best of it, and they alone can profit by it. I refer to the existence all through Australia and New Zealand of residential clubs, where male visitors can put up for any length of time instead of going to the dreary and generally deserted hotels of the city. An introduction by one or two members is of course indispensable, but having once obtained this, the lucky man is presented with "the freedom of the club" for all future time. This doubtless is the reason that the hotels in Sydney and even in Melbourne leave so much to be desired.

I must make a strong exception, however, in favour of the Esplanade Hotel at St. Kilda, one of the outskirts of Melbourne, where I had chosen to come to anchor rather than live in the crowded and hot city itself. The hotel has now passed into other hands, and is, I trust, as well conducted as it was by my host and his very pleasant, intelligent daughter.

So many people assured me that St. Kilda was extremely pretty, that I found myself at last repeating the formula from sheer laziness, but I do not think it at all pretty as a matter of fact. It boasts of an esplanade, a pier, and various sea-bathing establishments, but the water looked scarcely sufficiently inviting to tempt one to try the latter. I should, however, recommend any one to stay there sooner than in Melbourne during the hot summer months, for the sake of the cool breezes; and the numerous trains which take you into the city in ten to fifteen minutes prevent any feeling of isolation.

The gay time in Melbourne is the first week in November, when the famous races take place, and a very pandemonium of balls, picnics, and theatre parties sets in. The whole month is more or less given up to pleasure, a sort of carnival time of enjoyment (?); after which many of the Melbourne young ladies seem to collapse, and spend a hard-earned week or fortnight in their beds.

I came in for the fag end of the gaieties, in the shape of an invitation to a very pretty dance on board the *Nelson*. Special trains took us down to Williamstown, at the mouth of the harbour, where the ship lay, and from six to seven hundred guests mustered on board during the afternoon.

Every one who has danced on board a big "man-of-war" knows what a fairy-like scene can be produced where flags and flowers abound; but I had accepted the invitation more especially in order to see something of Melbourne society on a big and more select scale than is possible in Government House, where practically every one is welcomed to the weekly receptions. I noticed many well-dressed women, and some very pretty ones. At all afternoon entertainments there must be an undue proportion of women to men, especially in a busy money-making city, but this would not account for a fact which struck me very forcibly—namely, the very large amount of evident "duty-dances" that were going on. So many young and pretty "wallflowers" lined the side of the ship, whilst the more legitimate plant was seen whirling round in the rather limited space left for dancing.

In my perplexity I applied to a good-natured naval officer who had been introduced to me.

"Duty dances—money. Father and mother have good houses and give good dinners. The difficulty is to get men to come to a dance at all nowadays. A man has only two hands, and those are dipped deep in the money-bags out here. He has not a third arm to throw round a girl's waist at a ball. You don't catch a canny colonial wasting time that way," he answered.

A visit to Melbourne would be incomplete without going to the temporary cathedral, St. Paul's, to see and hear the surpliced choir of ten young ladies, who come into church as "sweet girl graduates," with white surplice, black hood, and tasselled college trencher complete. The singing was fair, but hardly good enough to justify the eccentricity.

When a venerable pillar of the Church, of over seventy-five, takes to himself a young wife under twenty years of age, I suppose it must be expected that she should indulge in some such vagaries *pour passer le temps*. The young lady headed the procession, and seemed very proud of her trencher.

Tourak is one of the most fashionable suburbs of Melbourne, and must represent a large portion of its wealth. The houses are very handsome and well furnished, and if expensive carpets, curtains, tables, and chairs, can bring happiness, Tourak should be a perfect Paradise. The approach to Paradise, however, lies appropriately through Purgatory, for the roads in the neighbourhood are execrable, and full of holes and ruts.

Labour is doubtless prohibitive in price, but as I was jogged and jolted from house to house I marvelled that these rich people do not put down a big lump sum to place the roads in order, and pay even a heavy yearly subscription towards keeping them so.

Melbourne in mid-November was at first exceptionally cold for the spring, and the bitter winds made it hopeless for some poor consumptive patients to leave the house for days together. English doctors are too fond of sending a patient vaguely "to Australia," forgetting the great differences of climate over such large areas of ground.

Some parts of Australia, more especially Adelaide, are peculiarly suited for chest complaints, but Melbourne is the last place I should suggest for a *poitrinaire*. When the cold wind ceased, eight days of continued hot winds and sirocco set in, most irritating to the nerves and enervating to the system. Doctors should take more trouble to acquaint themselves with the real climate of the various localities to which they send their patients, otherwise it means too often an acceleration of disease as well as death in a strange land.

It would be absurd to attempt anything like an exhaustive description of the Australian Colonies on the strength of my brief visit to them. At the same time, there is a good deal to be said in favour of " first impressions " both as regards people and places. Superficial as the grounds for forming these may appear, they have a curious knack of justifying themselves in the end. " *On revient à ses premières idées* " is at least as true as the more hackneyed proverb, " *On revient à ses premiers amours.*" My own first impressions were so strong that I sent home my biggest trunk the first week of my visit to Australia, feeling quite sure that I should not wish to prolong this indefinitely.

Being of a cautious nature, and having left England with the idea of spending possible months in Australia, I cannot quote a better proof of how far the reality disappointed my expectations.

Perhaps it is unfair to measure the country by any severe standard, and it may be justly urged, " Why not judge Australia at least as leniently as we judge of the virtues and failings of America ? Both are young countries, and equally deserving of forbearance on this score."

It seems to me the difference is as the difference between a youth who is vain but intelligent and a youth whose chief claims to consideration rest at present upon a well-filled banking account and an irrepressible self-appreciation.

Possibly the days are at hand when money-making for its own sake will begin to pall, and colonials will then wake up to the eternal fact that man does not live by bread alone—no, nor even by curtains, nor carpets, nor tables and chairs—and that money after all is chiefly valuable when it procures for us, and enables us to procure for others, the real meat and drink of spiritual and intellectual life.

CHAPTER III.

NEW ZEALAND.

First impressions of New Zealand—The Bluff—Invercargill—Lake
Wakatipu—Hector Mountains—Glenorchy—Kawarra Falls—Shot-
over River—Conversation with the Governor of Pentridge Gaol—His
ideas of heredity with regard to crime—Mr. Birley of Glenorchy—
Diamond Lake—Paradise—Ride to the valley of the Rees—Dunedin
—Happiness of married life in the Colonies as compared with
England—A visit to the Bishop of Dunedin—His home and
orphanage—Port Chalmers—A week on a sheep-station—Station life
—Sheep-shearing—The rabbit plague—System of extermination—
Christchurch—Its public buildings—River Avon—A Christchurch
sermon—A trip to the Sounds—Fishing—The New Zealand bush—
The *Flora*—Milford Sound—A modern Crusoe—Regatta in George's
Sound—An exciting race—Visit to a member of the New Zealand
Parliament—Wellington—Its buildings and climate—A stormy
passage to Auckland—Onehunga—Maori fortifications—Expeditions to Pink and White Terraces—*Sophia*—Sulphur baths—Advice
to ladies visiting hot Tarawera—Appearance of the Terraces since the
eruption—A thorough Christian—Visit to a Maori chief—A solitary
Englishman—New Zealand politics.

ON Wednesday, December 7th, I left my anchorage at
the Esplanade Hotel, St. Kilda, and sailed in the Union
steamship *Wairarapa* for New Zealand, intending to disembark at the first harbour, "the Bluff," and make my
way thence to the Lake district.

After what the colonials would call "an exceptional experience" in the way of a smooth passage, we sighted land early in the morning of December 11th, passing the snow-clad peaks of the south-west range of mountains, beyond which lie the world-famed New Zealand Sounds; and by 5 P.M. we were alongside the wharf at "the Bluff."

I had heard such dismal accounts of the Bluff, and had been warned so constantly not to judge the whole country by a first impression of rain and wretchedness, that it was quite an agreeable surprise to find the reality so far superior to my anticipations.

The Bluff, seen as I saw it first, on a fine bright summer evening, seemed quite a pretty little township. A few neat white houses, some rather bare green hills rising behind them, a signal-station keeping guard on the highest peak, low-lying hills stretching far away to east and west of us, —this was my first impression of New Zealand.

As the ship was to lie in harbour all night, I had arranged to land next morning, when several fellow-passengers came with me to spend the day at Invercargill, whence they would return to the ship, which sailed for Dunedin that evening.

Invercargill is an absolutely uninteresting town, lying eighteen miles from the Bluff, an hour's journey in a very slow train.

The streets are laid out on a very large scale, and the Invercargillites must be very hopeful people if they expect to fill in the flesh of such a huge skeleton. The finest buildings here, as elsewhere, are the grand stone banks, suggesting unlimited financial possibilities, which, I fear, are scarcely justified by the present condition of affairs in New Zealand.

Going on by train next day to Kingston, *en route* for Lake Wakatipu, the wearisome pace made one easily believe the story of the man only lately arrived in New Zealand who, being asked to take a train, declined with thanks on the plea that "he was in a hurry," and preferred walking.

The country at first was most flat and dull, relieved only by "tussocks" of grass, some green and some yellow, dried up and withered. The sheep will only eat the tussocks when green and fresh; so the old shoots are continually burnt down to make room for the tender undergrowth. We passed a great deal of the handsome New Zealand flax, so different in appearance from our own. It grows here to a height of several feet, and looks like bundles of rushes with a very handsome deep reddish-brown blossom. The cabbage-tree also abounds. It is a species of palm, growing on the top of a bare tree-stem with creamy and brown seeds.

Presently, to our left, appeared the snow-clad mountain range of Te Anan, beyond which lie the lakes of Te Anan and Manarowri. The scenery became much grander towards the last hour, and by one o'clock we reached the Kingston wharf, and embarked on the *Mountaineer*, a

convenient little steamer that plies up and down Lake
Wakatipu on certain days in the week. Salmon trout is
found in great quantities in this lake, averaging from nine
to thirty pounds in weight.

The first view of the deep blue waters of the lake is very
beautiful, but the mountains at this end are bare and bleak
without being extremely grand, and the scenery is rather
disappointing until, just before reaching Queenstown, the lake
opens out very much.   On the right hand side runs the
range of Hector Mountains, culminating in a line of weird
jagged   precipices,   called   "the   Remarkables,"   and   in
pleasant contrast lies the little township nestling between
the mountains, a gorge at her back and the lapping waters of
the intensely blue lake at her feet.

Fortunately for me, the landlady of the hotel at Glenorchy
(the head of the lake) was on board the steamer, and we
made great friends, especially when she found that I was
coming on in a few days to her house.   Visitors make the
greatest mistake in confining their stay on Lake Wakatipu to
a few days at Queenstown, with a run to Glenorchy by steamer
and back in a day.   All the finest scenery is at the head of
the lake, and can only be reached by riding or driving twelve
to twenty miles beyond Glenorchy. Mrs. Birley told me that
Miss Bird had stayed with her at Glenorchy many years
ago, before she achieved her Rocky Mountain fame.   "Such
a quiet little body ; I would never have dreamed she could
write like that," said my friend, describing her plain skirt and

little Turkey red twill garibaldis"—as though they might be calculated to have some disastrous effect upon literary ability!

I was at Lake Wakatipu rather early in the season, and found few travellers at " Eichardt's," supposed to be the best hotel, and a very comfortable house.

Underbred colonials are a very unpleasant experience. They stare at one as if one had come out of a menagerie, and the absence of simplicity on the one hand, and of *savoir faire* on the other, causes them to relapse into a sullen, sulky silence, most trying to the nerves of a solitary traveller.

Driving is an expensive amusement all over the Colonies. I was charged ten shillings for a short drive of barely two hours in a tiny buggy, holding only one person besides the driver.

I went one afternoon to the Kawarra Falls, a rapid at the outlet of the lake where it forms the River Kawarra, which lower down joins and becomes merged in the Klutha River. We passed a very pretty place belonging to Mr. Boyes, who was staying at Eichardt's Hotel when I was there. He has been quite ruined, poor man, by the rabbit pest, and obliged to give up his place, which was once one of the most prosperous in this part of the country. Further on we came to the Shotover Bridge, spanning part of the wide bed of the Shotover River. Half of this is a bed of sand and very treacherous quicksand too. In 1878 a tremendous flood caried off a splendid clover field, converting it into waste ground.

F

In this same year all the lakes rose, flooding the country, and boats could come into our hotel, which lies close to the lake. A severe winter with heavy snows on the mountains was followed by an early and hot spring, which melted the snow too rapidly, thus causing the lake waters to overflow.

Beyond Shotover lies the handsome building of the Frankton Hospital, and a wide expanse of agricultural country some 2,000 feet above the sea line, known as the Crown lands, where all the best crops of wheat and oats are raised.

Gum-trees seem to flourish as well here as in Australia, but they impoverish the ground by sucking up so much moisture and throwing out such distant roots. No crops will grow within seven or eight feet of a gum-tree plantation on this account. I strolled one afternoon to the " Park," a pretty tongue of land by the lake side, which has been planted with young shrubs.

Feeling very much like Robinson Crusoe on his desert island, I found my " man Friday " here. He appeared in the shape of a grey-headed elderly man with whom I had some pleasant and interesting conversation, and who turned out to be a Mr. Gale, governor of the Pentridge Gaol near Melbourne, a post he had held for thirty years. When I met him he was at the beginning of a six months' holiday; his health having at length broken down under the great strain and responsibility of his work.

He had served with Price (made famous under a *nom de*

plume in *For the Term of His Natural Life*), and was with him when he was killed. Many people affirm that this terrible tale is below rather than beyond the truth. Mr Gale, however, speaking from the official point of view, says that the book contains gross exaggeration. He maintains that Price was a really humane man, although severe, as was necessary with " men who were more like wild beasts than anything human." " What can you do without bolts and bars and with a few men in authority over hundreds of these wild animals, for that is what most of them were in the old convict days ? " It is a sad problem, and no doubt here as elsewhere there are two sides to the question. Still, there must have been terrible temptations to cruelty in the days when moral discipline was far less understood and practised than in our own time, and when there was no public opinion to restrain or criticize the use of physical force. Mr. Gale and I had some interesting talk on the subject of heredity with regard to crime. He says that, after an experience of thirty years, he is convinced that crime is as much inherited as drunkenness or insanity.

He said, " It is only of late years that people are coming to realize this, but it has been so from the beginning. During an experience stretching over thirty years I have never known one real criminal reformed for any length of time, although I have known several who have been clever enough to deceive my chaplains, some of whom have had considerable knowledge of criminal human nature. I do not

mean to say that a man who comes into gaol once or even
twice, tempted beyond his strength or through pressure of
unfortunate circumstances, may not reform and outlive all
prison taint; but from the real criminal class, I have never
known one reformation that was both genuine and lasting.
It is born and bred in the bone."

This seems a terribly sad conclusion, but once convinced of
the truth of it, surely we had better face facts, and try to
reform at the other end. I suggested that criminals should
not be allowed to marry, and so go on providing inmates for
asylums and gaols.

"No doubt," said Mr. Gale, "it must come to that some
day as a mere question of political economy, but at present
the world is not prepared for such extreme measures and
would not tolerate them."

If, as scientists now believe, the child before birth can be
as strongly influenced mentally by the condition of the
mother as it can be physically, is it visionary to imagine that
a child, conceived by parents given up to every bad passion,
should make its appearance in the world as much marked
morally by the mother's wicked impulses and desires as it
might be physically by her craving for any special food or
drink?   It is considered blasphemous and improper to speak
of these things, but is it not folly to ignore them and try to
" tinker up " at the wrong end, spending thousands of pounds
annually to support and chastise the criminals who should
never have been born?

After a few days in Queenstown, I started by steamer for
the head of the lake. The mountains became more bleak
and bare as one went further north, and the snow-clad peaks
of Mount Earnshaw and the Cosmos and Forbes ranges
soon came into sight. The whole of Lake Wakatipu is
famous for its gold gulches. In 1863 there was a regular
" rush " here, and gold has been found in greater or less
quantities ever since. The work is very hard, but the
excitement is proportionately great, and sometimes from £300
to £400 a week has been made by successful mining.

My host at Glenorchy, Mr. Birley, is considered to have a
very good " scent " for gold, and has done a great deal of
successful mining in his day. He is a man of good birth and
of considerable literary attainments, but no doubt spent his
money " not wisely but too well" in the old country, which
he left nearly thirty years ago. He had been much in
sporting and musical circles in those days, and having a
capital memory delights in talking about them. We had
many pleasant talks, but the conversation became a little
difficult occasionally, as he was constantly asking after
musical and dramatic stars, or celebrated racers who had
flourished when I was in my cradle.

The most beautiful expedition from Glenorchy is to
Diamond Lake, and a lovely place called Paradise—and well
deserving of the name—some ten miles from Glenorchy.
Mrs. Mason, wife of the present owner of the land, came
out and gave me a most kindly welcome and a cup of

excellent tea. She is a most refined and well-read woman. Her little drawing-room was full of reviews and books and papers, but she has led this strangely solitary life for years, and does not seem at all discontented. Her one complaint is that living so many miles from any possible medical aid might be fatal to her husband, no longer a young or strong man. After tea she took me a walk over some ploughed fields to a hill whence we had a most magnificent view of the snow-clad peaks of the Cosmos range of mountains.

The approach to Paradise was anything but reassuring, for we had to cross and recross the river many times, and our shaky conveyance was often half full of water.

Another day Mr. Birley and I took an unusually long ride of nearly forty miles in all to the valley of the Rees River, thence through a deep fern gully of interminable length, and up a steep mountain track to the quartz mining of the "Invincible Mill." The view thence was glorious, but nothing could surpass Paradise, and as my horse was extremely obstinate and had no mouth, I should have regretted the expedition with any companion less interesting than Mr. Birley, who discoursed upon every conceivable subject, from the Derby winner of 1846 to the poetry of Burns and Tennyson.

"For goodness sake, Birley, leave that nonsense alone, and take a rake to the garden, do," was the rather irreverent comment of his practical wife, when she came in one morning, and found him deep in Shakespeare's sonnets, which he was reciting to me.

"You see my poor dear wife's limited range of thought," he said, but took the hint, and, I am bound to say, did a good morning's work when once safely started. He is fortunate in possessing such a practical, hard-working wife, and appreciates the fact thoroughly.

I left them both with many regrets after a stay of three days, and retraced my steps by steamer and rail to a junction called "The Elbow," whence I took the Waihemo Plains railway to Dunedin.

The scenery was most monotonous, and the journey, of less than 200 miles, occupied twelve hours. Every one had spoken to me of the "Grand Hotel" at Dunedin as the finest in the Colonies. That may be, but it leaves much to be desired. It is built on a very large scale, somewhat resembling a baby American hotel. The food is pretentious but not well served, and the service generally is deficient. A smaller house would have served all purposes, and the money saved might have been well laid out in procuring greater comfort for the guests in other ways.

Dunedin is a much scattered and rather perplexing town. It is bounded on one side by a peninsula running right out into the sea, the bay being inclosed between this and the curve of the opposite shore. Dunedin proper stretches far away into the suburbs of St. Kilda, Caversham, &c., &c. There are some very severe hills in the town, but cable cars make locomotion easy. On the high promontories are some handsome houses belonging to the *élite* of the place, and commanding lovely views of the harbour. Dunedin is essentially a Scotch town. The Scotch overrun this part of the world as the Irish overrun America. The climate is much like that of England—nearly as much rain, but a good deal more sunshine—and, on the whole, I thought quite the pleasantest weather that I can look back upon during my three months' stay in New Zealand. I spent a week in Dunedin, and made many pleasant acquaintances, having brought letters of introduction from kind friends in Australia.

I think most English people will feel, as I did, far more at home in New Zealand than in Australia. There is less pretension and more simplicity of life, and the result is that people are more genial and natural.

As countries become more civilized, I fear the old instincts of hospitality are very apt to die out. This is inevitable. As a country develops, more strangers flock to it. Hotels are built, and take the place of private entertainment. The rare visitor who was once so eagerly greeted and so hospitably received, bringing as he did the atmosphere of the dear old country with him, is now spoken of as a "globe-trotter" and a "sponge." Telegraphs and steam communication of five weeks have put people out here "in touch" with England in a way which enables them to dispense with the society of the tourist unless he has some exceptional qualities to recommend him to their notice.

Much, no doubt, has been gained, but something also has been lost since the old instincts of hospitality have died out. In New Zealand, however, much of the ancient tradition still exists, and this doubtless accounts for the home-like feeling one experiences out here.

Amongst other introductions in Dunedin, was one to Mr. Gray Russell, who is well known in the town, and has a beautiful home situated on a road which skirts the harbour.

Having understood that I could reach the house by a sort of omnibus in about twenty minutes, I took my place one afternoon, intending to deliver my letter, pay a conventional ten minutes visit, and return within an hour or so. After jolting for more than an hour along the shore road, which seemed to roll itself out like a ribbon, we arrived at last at the gates of Mr. Russell's house. I had been told that a return vehicle would stop here in about half an hour, but wishing to be quite exact, made special inquiries of the driver. Imagine my horror when he calmly answered, "There is no other conveyance returning to Dunedin along the road till to-morrow morning." The people might be from home, and in any case were absolute strangers to me, and English tradition was too strong for me not to feel some qualms in such a dilemma. I "felt like" running away to hide in the bush, but remembered that food was a necessary factor for consideration.

"Can I not get a horse anywhere near here and ride

back?" I asked in my despair. "No, mum; nothing of
that sort to be had here," answered the man calmly
as he drove away; leaving me standing alone in the
road. There was nothing for it but to go boldly on, and
after mounting the hilly garden, which commands a lovely
view of the bay, to ring at the door bell. The moment
I entered and had confessed my sad plight, all my fears
were dispelled; a delightful hostess gathered in the position
at once, and within five minutes, she and I and a lady
calling there were laughing heartily over the adventure
and my despair.

Having to consult a doctor during my Dunedin visit,
and to wait over an hour in his room, gave me the chance
of a chat with an interesting fellow-patient, who afterwards
most kindly gave up her turn to me. She is now the wife
of a miller living up country, but was the daughter of an
old P. and O. sailing captain, and told me much of her
sea life. Having lost her mother as a baby, she had lived
up to the age of eighteen entirely at sea with her father,
being often away with him for two or three years at a
time.

"He was father and mother to me in one," she said. "He
taught me everything, and did everything for me." The
sad part of the story was that twelve years ago his ship
went down between New York and Liverpool, and he was
drowned. She and two sailors were the only survivors of
the wreck. His money unfortunately went down also, and

she would have been left penniless but for a pension allowed
her by the Company. She determined to come out to
New Zealand, wishing to see the country, and thinking the
change might do her good after the terrible grief and shock
of her catastrophe, and has found her fate here in the miller
aforesaid, who seems to make a kindly husband.

I may here mention a fact that has struck me as well as
many others during my colonial experiences. Prejudiced
as I may appear against the Colonies as a whole, I am bound
to confess that I never in the whole course of my life met
with so many happy married couples as in these countries.
The highest civilization (as, for instance, London life) does
not seem to be the most fertile soil for connubial bliss.
Possibly greater luxury, a more complex life, and, above all,
greater idleness, produce more grounds for divergence of
opinion and tastes. Station life in Australia, and life
generally in New Zealand, is far simpler than with us,
and interests are more in common and less likely to clash.
Add to this that in many cases there has been a hard struggle
to start with. Husband and wife have known what it is to
work hard, sharing a mutual life of labour and often of hard-
ship. When brighter days come, the tender memory of those
early struggles will remain to brighten their path, and
give the radiance to married love which, alas! so often
dies with the honeymoon in our own more pampered
existence.

Another pleasant day was spent in the beautiful home

of the Bishop of Dundin. He has designed his own house, which lies on high ground in a district called "The Waters of Leith," from a pretty stream which wanders down the valley. The lower half of the house is grey and white stone, the upper half red brick and dark wood, a curious but very effective combination.

Inside, the staircases, panelling, roofing, &c., are all of unpolished oak combined with a beautiful native wood of similar appearance. The bush in front of the house has been cut into pretty paths by the Bishop himself, and exquisite ferns of every description flourish here. The Bishop is full of taste and energy in adorning his own beautiful home, but does not forget to make others happy also.

In the afternoon I saw the orphanage which he and Mrs. Neville have started. They have built a pretty cottage behind their own house for some sixteen little girls, of ages varying from five to sixteen, such healthy-looking children! They were playing about on the steep wooden steps leading from the Bishop's house. "*Like Jacob's ladder with the angels upon it,*" was the Bishop's rather poetical remark as we passed.

It was very pretty to see the little pink sun-bonnets fluttering round him as he called out to them to join us. They needed no second bidding, but came clattering down, thrusting their little chubby hands into his, and begging him to make them a "bird's nest" of hay. It was quite sad to remember that he had no little birds of his own,

but these little orphan ones lie very near the episcopal
heart, I fancy.

I received no less than three kind invitations for what
would otherwise have been a solitary Christmas, and felt
quite grieved to be obliged to refuse two of them.

A few days later I started for a pleasant week's visit to
see something of "station life" on a sheep station within a
few hours by train of Dunedin.

My route lay past the beautiful harbour of Port Chalmers,
which is only seven miles from the town, and where all the
large steamers cast anchor.

The situation of this port is most beautiful, and as the sun
came out after a rainy afternoon, I saw it to great advantage.
Further on I got into conversation with a nice old couple who
had once owned a station near the one to which I was bound.
We had a long talk over New Zealand. The husband, like
every one else here who has any stake in the country, is down
upon democracy. I confessed that the Colonies would do
more than any other experience towards shaking my
anti-Conservative views. "Yes," he answered, "I am
not surprised to hear you say so. In England you are
only playing at democracy. Here you see it worked out,
and it means mob rule, with the result of ruin to the
country."

I cannot admit that this is the inevitable result of Liberal
moderate principles. To take refuge in Conservatism from
the *abuse* of Liberal principles is merely a compromise, and

therefore weak, as most compromises are apt to be. It is like
going in for total abstinence on the principle of confessing
that temperance is impossible.

The scenery was very pretty all the way to the junction,
where I changed into the local train which carries coal, &c.,
up to the little township near which my friend's station is
built. I think we took nearly an hour to get over this last
nine miles by train. My host arrived in a tiny buggy with
two horses, whilst I was arranging to leave my heavy baggage
in the station office. The formalities attendant upon this
very simple process were solemn enough for the signing of a
treaty, but at length I was free to jump into the carriage
and be whirled at a good pace along a mile of dusty road to
the pretty grey stone building, covered with green creepers
and yellow jasmine, which was to be my home for the next
few days.

The country around is very pretty, consisting of the undulating "spur and gully" form of hills so characteristic of
New Zealand; scarcely a tree to be seen, but excellent
pasturage for sheep. Round the house is a little plantation
of willow and eucalyptus, and a small orchard planted by
the owner.

We had several delightful drives for miles around in the
little buggy, drawn by two very "free" not to say skittish
horses; the only drawback to my perfect enjoyment being the
conviction that the "machine" must turn over before we
reached home in safety. It seems as if a breath of wind

might upset these very light little carriages, but doubtless this very quality of lightness is their salvation, for they bound over ruts and inequalities of ground in a truly surprising manner.

At first the weather was almost too cool for pleasant lounging, but soon the sun became deliciously warm, and to lie all morning in a long "deck chair," on the veranda, with a book in one's lazy hands, seemed the very acme of happiness to a poor travel-stained globe-trotter.

I saw comparatively little of my host, having arrived at shearing-time, the busiest time of year on a sheep station. However, there is always compensation to be had, and mine lay in the chance of going over the sheds with him, and watching the whole process of shearing, pressing, packing, &c. We came first to the pens where the sheep are kept ready for shearing after being "draughted in" from a common large pen. By an ingenious arrangement each sheep can be at once assigned to its pen as the flock passes up a narrow passage, one at a time. A door opening to the left will drive a sheep into a right-hand pen and *vice versâ*, the same arrangement higher up dividing other sheep of various species, to be determined in a moment by the brand. Thus special breeds are separated, and likewise the ewes, wethers, and lambs.

On this particular station there were about 20,000 sheep. Sixteen men were employed for the shearing, and each man should be able to shear about 100 sheep a day. It must be a very fatiguing process, bending over the sheep and keeping it in position, which is more than half the battle. I tried a little shearing on my own account, and could then better appreciate the skilful way in which the shears went through the wool, but alas! now and again the poor patient creatures get a bad cut. "As a sheep before her shearers is dumb." How forcibly those words came to my mind! When the fleece is removed, the dirty ragged edges are cut off, and it is rolled up and tossed into a special compartment according to quality. The wool of one kind is pressed down by a heavy "wool press" into a sack which is held out squarely for its reception. The pressure seems so great, and the bulk afterwards so solid, that it appeared impossible to compress it further. This, however, is done, and to a very considerable extent, for my host told me that these "two hundredweight" sacks became less than half their size through hydraulic pressure on board ship, before being lowered into the hold. Iron bands are then placed round the sacks, and the process is complete.

Some sheep-owners have the wool "scoured" before shipping, but the loss of weight entailed is generally considered too great in proportion to the extra price it fetches under these conditions.

The one drawback to my enjoyment of "station life in New Zealand" lay in the sad problem of rabbit extermination. Here it is brought home to one at every turn. The poor little innocent creatures who are such a terrible curse to the country scamper about under one's very feet, although on this one station from £500 to £600 a year are expended in the somewhat vain attempt to put them down.

The system of poisoning the rabbit holes is not only very costly, but seems horribly cruel. Two, three, and even up to five and six days have been known to elapse between the time when the poison was taken, and when the poor little victim has died after all these days of intolerable agony, for the phosphorescent poison literally burns them through and through.

The evil is on too gigantic a scale to be put down by shooting parties, and even this mode of killing is far from merciful in a country like New Zealand, which is full of hills and gullies. It is one thing to kill a few rabbits on the plain in England, giving a merciful knock on the head to supplement the shot when necessary, but it is quite another thing to shoot rabbits by wholesale on hilly ground or across gullies, where it is often impossible to get at them, and even when possible, men grow careless at length, and leave the poor little wretches to a lingering death, for familiarity breeds cruelty as well as contempt. No doubt it is unreasonable to expect that men who are being ruined year after year by the rabbit plague should cherish much tenderness of feeling towards the innocent causes of their woe, but this does not make the facts less bad from the rabbits' point of view.

I was told lately that the man who introduced rabbits

G

into New Zealand was still alive, and broken-hearted with remorse to think of the many men he had ruined by his rash action. I should feel quite as much remorse for the terrible torture inflicted upon the rabbits themselves. It made one long to be a great and successful chemist, and able to discover some merciful means of getting rid of the poor creatures.

Turning my back with many regrets on my pleasant "station" life, a hot, dusty, and uninteresting journey over the flat Canterbury plains, brought me one fine evening in early January to Christchurch, the literary centre of the Colony.

My hotel being situated in the Cathedral square, this was naturally the first building that attracted my attention. It is built of grey stone, and said to be modelled after one at Caen. The inside is plain but handsome, and possesses a little really good stained glass. The town is flat and very hot in summer, being built upon the plains, but it is full of interest owing to the beauty of the public buildings. These are of the same fine grey stone as the Cathedral, and are chiefly educational. The University Hall is very fine, but simple. It does not compare with the one at Sydney, but runs a very good second to it. Christchurch College is somewhat of a budding university, with a fine chapel and school-house, and a number of wooden houses round the square, where the masters live. But the Museum is the *ne plus ultra* of Christchurch, and the inhabitants have good cause to be proud of it. It would do credit to any large town in England or on the Continent. There is a fine collection of minerals and metals, skeletons of prehistoric animals, and a whole room full of the " Moa," a bird now extinct in New Zealand, but which was known here within the last hundred years. The skeleton looks something like an ostrich, but it is on a larger scale, and the legs look even stronger than those of an ostrich.

It is thanks to these strange birds that Christchurch possesses such a fine collection of other things, for the authorities have been constantly enabled to make valuable exchanges with other European collections by sending them specimens of the Moa, which is peculiar to this country.

The real pride and glory of the city, however, is the River Avon, which appears to be to Christchurch what "the harbour" is to Sydney.

It is more of a wide stream than a river, bordered on either side by deep waving willows which often interlace overhead, and is certainly very lovely and picturesque. A boating party on the Avon is a very pleasant and refreshing experience after a hot, dusty summer's day.

We had some terribly hot days during my week's visit, and the "sirocco" wind made any exertion irksome and life itself almost intolerable, but I was assured, as usual, that my experience was " *a most exceptional one.*"

Christchurch has some fine suburbs. One day we went

out by train and coach to Sumner, a seaside place with a bold coast-line and rocky scenery, about an hour from the town. Hotels and houses are built here, and it seems to be a summer refuge from the relaxing heat of the city.

In all New Zealand towns a curious habit obtains, viz. a Saturday evening " parade," when all the shopkeepers turn out and perambulate the streets for an hour or two. The crowd at Christchurch was great, and not very select, but it was an amusing experience for once.

I spent a happy Sunday with kind friends who own a handsome house in the suburb of Papanui, the invitation having been given for that special day that I might hear a famous preacher who ministers there. He struck me as clever, but scarcely sympathetic, and spoke of the "fall of man " as a " clumsily put together story, invented to account for the presence of evil in the world." The really curious thing was to note the strange advance in thought and the daring expression of it possible in these days, out of England at any rate. The congregation was composed of quiet, respectable men and women, who listened to these startling remarks without any display of surprise or emotion. In any large city where there is ample choice of theological food, such remarks might be made with impunity, for each congregation represents a special section of thought and opinion, but it seemed odd to listen to such a daring Bible commentary addressed to a country congregation, composed, as it must be, of so many various elements.

One of the most favourite expeditions in New Zealand is the "Sounds trip." The Union Steamship Company send one of their boats to make this trip once a year. The expedition can only be made in the month of January, when the clouds and mists have lifted off the mountains, which they envelope during the rest of the year. Hitherto the one trip had been found sufficient for the numbers wishing to undertake it, but on this occasion it was considered advisable to send the steamer to the Sounds twice, and so divide the large number of passengers whose names had been down in the Company's books for many weeks beforehand.

As it is impossible to do everything, even during a lengthy stay, my first intention had been to miss this expedition and cross the South or Middle Island to Graymouth, whence I trusted to get by steamer to Napier, but I found that this would entail waiting ten days for a steamer with miserable accommodation, unless I could face five consecutive days of very rough coaching, which, after American experiences, was an impossibility.

Being forced to modify my plans, I determined to go upon the "Sounds trip," which had been described to me in the most glowing colours as something far surpassing the wonders of the Norwegian fiords, with which I was already familiar.

There are two great classes of travellers, who might be described in slang terms as the "*the Crabbers*" and "*the Gushers*." The former never find anything to compare with places already visited; the latter have never beheld any

scene so marvellous as that upon which their eyes rest at
the moment.   Endeavouring to avoid both extremes, I can
strongly recommend the expedition, but it will not be an
unmixed delight to bad sailors, and fine weather is, of course,
a most important factor, and one that cannot be counted upon
with any certainty.

Our steamer, the *Tarawera*, started from Port Chalmers
carrying ninety-seven passengers. Our route lay past the
Bluff, and so to the west coast Sounds, and the roughness of
the passage upon this occasion quite justified its usual
character. Allowing for the passage to and from the Bluff
to Port Chalmers, and the rough seas to be encountered
between the haven of the various Sounds, I find a record of
four and a half days' sea-sickness to be deducted from the
ten days' pleasure !

For a pleasure-trip this is rather depressing, and it is
well for bad sailors to count the probable cost in discomfort before starting.   The cost in money is wonderfully
moderate. Twelve pounds covers all expenses, and the food
and accommodation are fairly good.

Many of our fellow-passengers were extremely pleasant
and sociable, and dances, concerts, and recitations beguiled
the evenings, and had been all planned and arranged beforehand through the energy and kindness of the ship's officers.
In fact some of the young ladies seemed to look upon these
entertainments as the *raison d'être* of the expedition rather
than its supplement; and I was occasionally amused by the

way in which picnics and expeditions on shore were apt to
be cut short, because some one "*must go back to the ship
to practise a song or rehearse a part.*"

It is useless to go into any detailed account of these
glorious inlets of the sea. Those who know them by
experience will require no description, and to those less
favoured, continuous word-painting is generally ineffectual
and apt to become wearisome.

We had three fine days to start with, two of which were
spent in exploring the wonders of the bush round Reservation
Inlet. The steamer anchors in the various Sounds, and a
steam-launch and several boats take the passengers for
land-trips, or on fishing expeditions, according to their
various tastes.

One boat will take all those wishing to fish to the most
likely spot for this sport. Another boat is filled with
enthusiastic sketchers. Others wish only to dawdle about
and picnic on shore, whilst the steam-launch is generally
patronized by those who want to get over a good deal of
ground (or rather of water) in a short time, to gain a general
impression of the Sound without the trouble of landing and
scrambling through the thick bush which comes down on all
sides to the water's edge.

I went on one fishing expedition, but never wished to
repeat the experiment, as my sporting instincts are too
rudimentary to enable me to look at the poor fish flapping
themselves to death in the boat, without a pang.

The fish in the Sounds are very varied in kind and numerous in quantity; almost too much so from the sportsman's point of view, I should imagine. Within an hour our boat was crowded up with fish of every sort, colour, and kind, and there seemed little need of skill, or chance for the display of it. The blue cod, and rock cod, were the best for eating, and we had constant supplies of these for our breakfast-table.

To me, the exquisite New Zealand bush formed the greatest attraction. It is impossible to penetrate this to any distance, as the thick, trailing, interlacing boughs and creepers form an insuperable obstacle, and the dense foliage becomes impenetrable within a short distance of the shore; but every inch of the bush here is beautiful. Every species of exquisite fern is to be found here, more especially the rare "kidney fern" which grows here in great profusion, shaped as the name denotes, and of the loveliest tender shade of green. The New Zealand honeysuckle, which is scarlet, with a leaf like mistletoe, and a species of myrtle with a red blossom, called the "Rata," are the most beautiful and conspicuous shrub and tree at this time of the year, but fresh beauties await one at every step. Perhaps the varied mosses strike one as much as anything. They are of every shape and colour. Some are like the softest tiny fairy cushions of yellow, green, and brown. One nook which we came upon by chance after a long scramble up some rising ground, was so beautifully carpeted with ferns and mosses of every description, that we, proud discoverers, called it Paradise at once, and could not rest until we had persuaded various friends to go through the tangled trees and up the steep ascent for the sake of such exquisite beauty. I trust that those who reach the real Paradise may drop some of the restlessness of human nature *en route*. The gentlemen looked round at our fairy palace, said, " Yes, awfully pretty," and in two minutes added, " Hadn't we better be moving off now ? " just as though they had not come some twelve thousand miles to see these very wonders !

I should describe the New Zealand Sounds as " lovely " rather than " grand," with the exception of Milford Sound, which is the culminating point of the whole trip, and most fully deserves the epithet. Unfortunately, as we steamed into Milford Sound, at 8 A.M., the clouds were very heavy, and at first almost hid from us the mountains which rise here, sheer and straight from the water, to heights varying from 2,000 to 5,000 feet. These bare rocks are covered with short green shrubs and ferns and foliage, growing apparently out of the living rock and with no chance of soil. Many small waterfalls pour down the rocky mountain-sides, the largest of these being 550 feet in height. Owing to the recent heavy rains, this waterfall was certainly seen to the greatest perfection, but it was difficult to realize the height as three times that of Niagara !

The New Zealand boats from Melbourne sometimes put

into Milford Sound before touching at the Bluff. If any
tourist can insure a passage on one of these occasions, he may
console himself by thinking that he has seen the most beautiful and characteristic spot in the whole "Sounds trip," and
this without the fatigue of being amused for ten days.

To have fine days, and to wander about an exquisitely
beautiful "bush," is as near an approach to Paradise as I can
conceive. But "to be amused" for ten mortal evenings seems
to me an equally vivid conception of Purgatory. This doubtless is the reason that picnics, which give immense trouble,
are rarely successful. To start upon a purely "pleasure-trip"
is almost invariably a fatal experiment, and I think it arises
from the great difficulty of "being amused to order." Pleasure
as a wayside flower is delightful, but pleasure planned to rule
has often the sickly, enervating atmosphere about it of a
hothouse plant.

One day, passing an island in George's Sound, the captain,
through his glass, saw a man with two dogs making
violent signs for us to "heave-to." Time happened to be an
object to us just then, but of course a boat was lowered at
once, and two or three sailors pushed off towards the shore.
We all, the captain included, imagined nothing less than a
Robinson Crusoe, or at least a starving man, but when the boat
returned with him we found he had no wish to be taken on
board, nor was he even in want of food. He had lived for
some months upon the island, shooting and skinning birds,
and only wanted some more pepper to carry on his work! As

the captain's humanity had cost him over an hour's delay, his language upon hearing this was anything but Parliamentary, and I fancy our modern Crusoe got all the pepper he wanted, in one way at any rate!

Before returning to Port Chalmers, a grand regatta was organized to take place in George's Sound, chiefly in the interests of the sailors. Numerous races were arranged for them, including the firemen, and it was pleasant to find that no less than £50 had been subscribed amongst us for the well-earned prizes, for officers and men alike do their very best to make this a pleasant time to every one on board.

One race consisted of three boats with four young ladies in each, representing, respectively, Christchurch, Wellington, and Dunedin, the prizes in this case to be pretty silver brooches, shaped like oars, with the name of the ship, *Tarawera*, engraved upon them. But the real excitement of the afternoon was the " Harrow boys *versus* Australians."

The latter were so very "superior" and so absolutely sure of victory, and the former so modest and so sure that they could not win, seeing that the Australians had already practised together whilst the Harrovians were a "scratch lot" (two of them over forty years of age) who had never rowed together before. As the Australians, moreover, had the best and lightest boat, and got the inside place in rounding the buoy which marked the turning point in the course, there seemed absolutely no hope at first for our poor Englishmen. They "played," however, a splendid "losing game," and actually won by sheer pluck, coming in first by about a quarter of a boat's length amidst the frantic cheers of all the English on board. It was far more exciting than any University race I ever saw rowed. I don't believe there was a penny upon the race. It was sheer patriotism with us all, and an overwhelming desire that the "old country" might hold her own against colonial "bounce." To my horror I saw one of the Harrovians (a delicate man) throw up his oar in the air before the winning-post was gained, and in my ignorance did not understand that this was done merely by way of claiming the race, because he had just noticed that the cox of the Australian boat had quietly leant forward and was pulling for the "stroke," who had given in. Fortunately the victory by this time was assured, but I was amused, when the English-man afterwards reproached his adversary for doing such a thing, to hear the latter reply quite calmly and evidently with no sense of shame: "Dear me, had you only just noticed it? *Why, I had been pulling for him half the time.*"

On our return to Port Chalmers I spent a few delightful days in the beautiful house overlooking Dunedin Harbour belonging to a member of the New Zealand Government. He and his charming and interesting wife gave me the kindest welcome, and a hospitality that sounds quixotic to our prosaic English ears. The house seemed literally to be made of india-rubber so far as the bedrooms were concerned at any rate, for in addition to a very large home party, strangers seemed to turn up at every meal, and to the last day of my stay I could never quite realize who was and who was not, sleeping in the house. When I mention the fact that the whole number of our fellow-passengers on board the *Tararera* were invited to a garden party on the afternoon of our return, it will give some idea of their princely instincts of hospitality—instincts, moreover, involving no inconsiderable amount of trouble where domestic service is on so small a scale compared with our own, and requires so much supplementing by the members of the household.

Taking another U. S. C. boat for Wellington, I left Dunedin on a day of drenching rain, and after spending some hours in Christchurch, where the vessel put in, reached Wellington on the second day, Friday, January 27th. There I was met by a kind friend and her husband, who had spent eight years in the town previously, and knew every nook and corner of it, a great advantage to the visitor of a few days.

The Wellington harbour carries off the palm, I think, even in this country of beautiful harbours. It is surrounded by high hills, and the entrance is quite concealed, giving the effect of a lovely large lake. The town is very hilly, and almost entirely built of wood, including Government House, the Houses of Parliament, and the Government buildings, said to be the largest wooden buildings in the world. Parliament was adjourned at the time of my visit, so I had no opportunity of comparing matters here with the Australian Houses of Legislation.

The favourite expedition from Wellington is to the Lower Hutt, a distance of ten miles by rail, along a very beautiful sea-coast line. In McNab's gardens, a mile from the station, we found some specimens of very rare palms and other trees, and also a number of the "Nekau" palms. In these latter, the leaves grow only at the very top of the tree, but about half-way up is a band of scarlet seeds dropping from the circle of the tree-trunk.

The Wellington climate, during my short experience, struck me as extremely relaxing, and a young lady friend with whom I went later to the hot springs, and who had spent five months in this town, fully indorsed my opinion. The Wellington wind is proverbial. It is said that you can always recognize a Wellington man in any quarter of the globe, by the way in which, from long habit, he will always walk about clutching his hat with one hand! It is still worse for an unfortunate woman, but every one is in the same plight, and one has to become reconciled at last to being literally blown into a friend's house with touzled hair, hat or bonnet coming off one's head, and a wisp of gown and petticoat impeding the "pilgrim's progress."

Making a very good second to my terrible experience between Hobart and Sydney, comes the recollection of our passage from Wellington to Auckland in the *Takapuna*, a boat originally constructed simply as a mail-boat, 900 tons, with engines of 2,000 horse-power! The shaking and plunging under these circumstances can be better imagined than described. I believe one would have suffered on such a boat in almost any sea, but we came in for a stormy night on the north-east coast of the North Island. Even the stewardess succumbed, and said she had never closed her eyes all night.

About noon of the following day we reached the desolate-looking township of New Plymouth, and anchored there to land cargo, a quiet hour of rest between the beginning and ending of our misery.

On the second day out, at 8.20 A.M., we made Manakau Harbour, and landed at Onehunga. Three-quarters of an hour by train took us across the narrow tongue of land dividing this harbour from Auckland, where we put up, and found comfortable quarters at the well-known Star Hotel. Here at long last, after an eight months' search, I found my travelling companion, who had recently returned from Samoa. It was quite a case of "Livingstone and Stanley" taken with female parts. However, by this time, I had a young lady with me who wished to see the hot lake district before returning to England, so it was settled that my other friend should return to Sydney, leaving us to follow at our leisure. A few days of rest in Auckland gave me the chance of seeing something of the town, which is very hilly, as is the case with all New Zealand towns. The shops are good and handsome, and we were especially delighted with the Public Library, which is in every respect excellent, and to which Sir George Grey's collection forms a great addition.

A long and beautiful drive in the company of a gentleman who had been born and lived all his life in the Colony gave us the chance of seeing the various places where our troops had been encamped during the Maori War. There are numerous hills of volcanic origin around Auckland, and these were cut out into fortifications during the war by the natives. We drove all round the bay, and across the narrowest part of North Island from Onehunga to Auckland, passing the site of the old barracks, which were situated close to the present Public Library. The most celebrated spot near Auckland is Mount Eden, the bourne of all holiday-makers and every tourist. From the top of this steep hill a magnificent view of the harbours of Auckland and Manakau and of the whole "lie" of the country can be obtained.

Of course the district of the Pink and White Terraces affords little to interest the traveller since the terrible volcanic eruption of 1886. Still, we felt bound to go and see for ourselves "how little remained to be seen," and I do not regret the expedition. The "geysers," at any rate, remain as they were, and, having been over the Yellowstone Park in Wyoming, it was interesting to me to be able to compare the two districts.

Moreover, the mosquitoes at the Star Hotel were becoming

rampant, and we fondly clung to the hope of leaving them behind us there.

We left Auckland one morning at 8 A.M., and after a dreary and uninteresting journey, reached Oxford, our resting-place for the first night, at 4.30 P.M., and found a pleasant quiet inn there. Being a very nervous sleeper, and having passed many nights of mosquito misery, I put our hostess through a regular catechism, much to the amusement of my friend. Our little whitewashed rooms looked into a square sort of yard, where cocks and hens abounded, and a huge dog was disporting himself amongst them. "Have you many mosquitoes here?" I asked first, with a lively recollection of past tortures. "Do the cocks crow *very* early in the morning?" "Does your dog bark *all* night long?" I believe the woman thought I was a harmless lunatic being "taken around" for my health, but I felt that it was so easy, when a fellow-sufferer, to sympathize with poor Carlyle's nervous and apparently foolish dread of anything on the earth beneath or in the heavens above that could by any possibility disturb his night's rest. Only those who know by bitter experience the torture of constant sleepless nights, should be allowed to criticize the poor Chelsea philosopher on this point.

Next morning we were up and off by coach at 7.30 A.M. for Ohinemutu on Lake Rotorua. Our way led through a very beautiful bush, full of the lovely tree-fern and many other specimens, notably the one called Prince of Wales's feathers, which is very rare, growing only in one spot of this

H

bush. It is very feathery and graceful, from one to two feet in height and about six or seven inches wide. We reached the Lake House at Ohinemutu at 12.30, having changed our driver *en route*, and being severely shaken and jolted in consequence, for the road was much the same all along our journey. The horses seemed to recognize in a moment the difference of hand. I could scarcely have believed that a driver could have so much power in his hands to save or to inflict suffering, although I can remember a similar experience in the Yosemite Valley.

This district is famous for sulphur and other medicinal baths, and as there are bath-houses attached to the hotel, we were glad to avail ourselves of the luxury after our tiring drive, instead of going at once to the Sanatorium, which lies at some distance from the Lake House.

Next day, three of us started in a buggy for a long weary drive of twelve miles across a scorching country, to Tiketere, where the boiling black mud-pots are situated. These are quite as large as those in the Yellowstone Park, but do not possess the same beautiful colouring, being only black and the very darkest shades of brown. The sulphur fumes were almost unbearable, and we were glad to take shelter in a very neat and clean little *whare* or hut made of flax, belonging to our guide. Here we ate our lunch, and then walked up a steep hill to get a view, finally driving on to " Whakarewarewa," where we saw some geysers which delighted my companion, who had had no previous geyser experience, but seemed to me very small as compared with those in the Wyoming district. The charm of this unpronounceable place, however, lies in the glimpses one gets of Maori life and the native *whares*. The Maori element is dying out so quickly nowadays that it is only in such places as these that one comes across it.

We went to call upon the famous " Sophia," who was out at the time, but whom we met later in the afternoon—a bright and intelligent-looking woman of about fifty years of age. Since the destruction of the Terraces, poor Sophia's occupation is gone, for, as most of my readers will know, she was the guide to this district, and is not allowed to poach upon the preserves of geyser district guides. This is reasonable enough no doubt, but it seems hard that the poor woman should lose her employment whilst still in the full vigour of her strength. Her *whare* looked very clean and neat, the beds being arranged on the floor as in an Indian house. A bright boy of twelve, Sophia's youngest hope, was sitting on the floor when we came in, but his mother was not at home. One of us having a visiting card at hand, we wrote our names upon it, and left it rather as a joke. Sophia was quite equal to the occasion. We met her the same afternoon and had a little talk, saying we had been to her *whare*. Next day to our great amusement we were told that Sophia wished to see us, and we found her sitting in the passage, looking most dignified and composed. " I have come to return your call," she said, in the prettiest English, and with the bright

smile and little backward toss of the head which are so
characteristic of her. Her manners in their quiet dignity
and self-possession would do credit to any London drawing-
room, and I felt quite shocked when a gentleman of our
party suggested her going into the kitchen and asking for
some beer as a point to the interview! It seemed such a
terrible collapse, but she smiled, wrapping her shawl round
her with unconscious native grace, and took the hint, and I
have no doubt drank her beer with the air of an empress.

At the Sanatorium, which is much frequented, guests can
be taken into the house (on certain conditions) for two
guineas a week. The smell of sulphur would be too overpowering for many visitors; but to invalids, unable to walk
to and fro, such an establishment must be a great boon.

Of the various baths here, "the Priests" and "Madame
Rachel" are two of the most popular. The former is more
especially used for skin affections, and is said to produce an
eruption in many cases where it is not taken under medical
advice, so we carefully avoided this, but had more than one
"Madame Rachel" bath, which gives a very gentle and refreshing sensation, and leaves the skin for the time dazzlingly
white and soft.

Another day we were up early, and off by 8 A.M. to the
Waitapo Valley, a beautiful drive of more than eighteen miles
through bush and over fern-covered hills. The road, wonderful to relate, is excellent. We walked for some distance
up the valley to see a very beautiful small green lake, and

on our return journey climbed an easy fern gully to get a
view of Mount Tarawera and the scene of destruction. I
should strongly recommend this expedition to ladies, in place
of attempting the far more arduous, and for them less interesting, journey to the foot of the Terraces. The latter entails
a very rough ride of ten miles on horseback, then a row across
the lake of eight miles, and at the last only a view of the
rough crags and boulders that have fallen from the mountain-
side, and enveloped the reaches of ground where the beautiful
Terraces once existed. These are said to be forming again,
but had only reached about two inches in height when we
were there.

If a woman is strong enough to climb Mount Tarawera,
descend, and accomplish the return journey in the same day,
of course she can do so; but even strong men find their
strength severely taxed now that the conditions are so
entirely changed. In the Terrace days, the ride from
Ohinemutu to the foot of the lake was far easier than it
is now when partially destroyed by *débris*, and there was
then a house of rest and entertainment at the latter place,
from whence the mountain ascent could be made at leisure.

The fern gully I have mentioned was about five miles
from Waitapo on the return journey to Ohinemutu, where
we were staying. On emerging from it on to the grassy
hills we came upon a weird scene of desolation. Immediately
in front of us rose the white scarred sides of Mount Tarawera,
the crater which is on the side of it, distinctly visible and

still smoking. Many of the trees around are still white with the rubbish and deposit from the volcano, which poured forth lava for a distance of several miles at the time of the eruption. The ground all round the mountain was charred and whitened with volcanic deposits, and the famous Tarawera rose up grim and desolate and forbidding. Yet the whole weird scene held me with such fascination that I could scarcely tear myself away from it, when my companions had at length exhausted their curiosity. The site of the Terraces is on the further side of the mountain from where we saw it, but they are now absolutely ingulfed by the *débris* of the awful catastrophe. The glory of the district has certainly departed with them. I do not think it can now compare for interest with the Yellowstone Park. The geysers are far inferior both in number and size. The mud-pots, although large, do not approach in beauty to those in Wyoming, simply because they have no charm of colour, whereas the latter give you every varying shade from faintest cream to deepest rose and red, and there is nothing now here worthy to be mentioned for natural beauty with the glorious Yellowstone Cañon. On the other hand, however, the native Maori element makes such a place as the geyser district of Whakarewarewa far more interesting in many ways than Wyoming.

On our return to Auckland we made friends with a very delightful man, the head of a South African brotherhood, who had come to New Zealand for a year's change after his arduous missionary labours at his responsible post. He was

one of the brightest, most simple-minded and most
joyous "Christians" it has ever been my good fortune to
meet, full of sympathy for the pleasures and lives of others
differing so entirely from his own, and absolutely free from
any tinge of "superiority" in manner or thought. He
seemed to me to recognize far more deeply than most people
are able to do, that the world is made up of various elements,
and that the best possible life for one man may be the worst
possible life for another. Himself a celibate, but without a
touch of asceticism, I fancy few young people would find
truer counsel or more loving sympathy with the marriage
state than with him—so long as it was a case of "true
marriage," and not a mere conventional bargain.

We went with him one morning to Auraki, across the
harbour from Auckland, to see a Maori settlement and
"Chief Paul," a smiling, grizzled fat old chief of sixty-two,
who reigns here supreme. The latter showed us with great
pride a wonderful native war canoe made from the trunk of
a tree. It is eighty feet wide, and is capable of holding fifty
natives, who propel it by small single paddles on either side.
He told us that it had raced the gig of the *Nelson* man-
of-war, but we were left in doubt as to which won, and
were too polite to ask. The chief's house is distressingly
European-looking, a neat little white wooden cottage with
green blinds and a regular "best parlour" for the sitting-
room.

We had some talk with an old Englishman (Rogers by

name) who was sitting on a bench in the sun. He has lived here alone for some years, not able to speak a word of Maori, and being the only European amongst them. Communication must be carried on by signs, for even the chief can barely pronounce one or two English words. The poor old man seemed quite content to end his life in these queer surroundings. He keeps a few chickens and a pig, and manages to support himself in some mysterious way. He has sons in the Colonies, but has lost sight of them. "They don't care to look me up, for fear I should want something from them," said the poor old man. It seemed very hard that they should leave him to live and die amongst these natives.

Froude has written so powerfully and exhaustively upon the financial position of New Zealand, that it would be absurd to attempt any supplement to or comment upon his remarks. But as I only propose to give my "impressions" for what they are worth, I cannot quit the subject of New Zealand without recording the strongest one of all—namely, that *righteousness* (in its literal sense of right-doing) is (putting matters on the lowest ground) incomparably the "best policy."

In no country in the world, I think, does this old copy-book morality stand out in such letters of living fire, nor does Matthew Arnold's "law that makes for righteousness" teach us more plainly what are even the temporal penalties of ignoring it.

The political corruption and the consequent bankrupt condition of the country speak for themselves. Here, where politicians are paid servants to the Government, and have, moreover, much to gain besides their seats, to be a "member of the House" is not only a laudable ambition but a very decided worldly advantage, and in too many cases it is practically *bought*. A man lets his constituents understand that if elected he will obtain a grant of Government money to be expended in that special district. This is too often spent upon perfectly useless improvements—railways that nobody requires, or bridges that nobody uses. I have myself seen bridges which had been in course of construction for years, the early part of the work absolutely rotting before the latter part was finished. As nobody seemed to want the bridge when completed, this was of minor importance. The great object seemed to be, that money should be spent in the town or district, so that each man might have a better chance of "pickings," and making his own "little pile" out of the general sum of useless expenditure. The result of this policy is that the country is now in a rotten financial condition, and men are at last waking up to the fact that the interests of the individual cannot in the long run be divorced from the interests of the community, and that St. Paul's command, "Look not every man on his own things, but every man also on the things of others," is quite as sound a maxim in political economy as it is in Christianity.

CHAPTER IV.

VIÂ CHINA TO JAPAN.

A shaky boat—The Bay of Islands—Sydney once more—A visit to Queensland—A month at Eton Vale—Life on a head station— Brisbane—Off to China—A delightful steamer—Townsville— Tropical heat—Port Darwin—Torres Straits—The Philippines— Hong Kong Harbour—Beauties of the town—Canton—A hospitable friend—Pagodas and bazaars—A Chinese cemetery—Visit to a Chinese family "at home"—Deformed feet a mark of social standing —Chinese babies—The mosquito plague—The Peak at Hong Kong— A coolie "strike"—The far-famed P. and O. line—Shanghai—The Cathedral—Crops and climate—A strange conveyance—Visit to a Chinese orphanage—Chinese commercial morality—The Chinaman " not so black as he's painted "—Chinese civility *versus* Irish insolence.

My return voyage from New Zealand to Australia was a far more bitter experience than the trip from Melbourne to the Bluff had been three months previously.

This time we sailed from Auckland direct to Sydney in a very good but extremely "shaky" boat, the *Rotomahana*. It was not reassuring to hear that bets were constantly made· on board her that even on the calmest day no man could hold a glass of wine in his hand without spilling it, owing to the unusual amount of vibration.

The law of compensation, however, worked even here, for

the *Rotomahana* has the very kindest captain in the world (Carey), who seems to be universally popular. We reached Russell and the Bay of Islands early on the morning after our start, and had a pleasant walk whilst the ship remained for coaling. The Bay of Islands is extremely beautiful, a small edition of the Thousand Islands on the St. Lawrence.

We will draw a veil over the next few days of misery (relieved only by the extreme kindness and thoughtful care of our captain), and, passing over a happy week spent with kind friends in Sydney, I found myself by the end of February *en route* for a visit to Queensland by the newly opened railway. A rail between Sydney and Brisbane had been partially open for some time, but the entire connection had only recently been made; thus sparing the very rough passage by sea to those who, like myself, are extremely bad sailors.

I left Sydney at 5 P.M., crossing the beautiful Hawkesbury River in a steam ferry by moonlight, and getting at once into the "sleeper," in which I had engaged my berth beforehand. Armadale was reached by noon next day, after passing through a part of the country called New England, where the atmosphere was cool and pleasant, even during this summer month. The scenery all along this line is beautiful, quite surpassing anything I had yet seen in Australia, with the exception, of course, of such districts as the "Blue Mountains."

We passed thousands of gum-trees, naturally, but these

were diversified by hills and reaches of excellent pasturage. The extreme *greenness* of the latter, in spite of the hot summer weather, struck me very much, and was suggestive of heavier rains here than elsewhere. Not wishing to arrive at my friend's house in the dead of night, I had arranged to sleep at Warwick, a quaint little commercial town, from whence three hours by train next day, over the famous Darling Downs, brought me in safety to Cambooya, a little railway-station within two miles of the well-known Queensland "head station" of Eton Vale.

The property is owned by Sir Arthur Hodgson, whose name will be familiar to most readers as having been, with Sir Patrick Jennings, one of the earliest pioneers of Queensland. A son of Sir Arthur is the present manager of the estate, and he and his wife (an old friend of mine) were my kind and hospitable host and hostess during a very happy month of rest and enjoyment in their beautiful home.

I fancy the house at Eton Vale must often bring a shock of pleasant surprise to those who enter its hospitable walls expecting the typical "station" of whitewashed walls and scanty furniture, and find a perfectly appointed English home, artistic and beautiful, even to its smallest detail. The single story and the wide twelve-foot veranda all round the house alone reminded one that this was Queensland, and not a charming country house in England.

A large head station is like a small village. It possesses its own school for the children of those employed on the station, various cottages for what we should call "the labourers" on the estate, "boundary riders," &c., and a comfortable wooden hut to receive any stray travellers who may arrive at any hour of the day or night. The hospitality of a head station includes a night's lodging to any one who asks for it, and a regular allowance of rations, so much meat, bread, tea and sugar, &c., to each individual. Remarking that this boundless hospitality must be a severe tax, my host explained to me that here as elsewhere there are two sides to a question, and that often they were glad to keep a "sun downer" for a week or two when extra hands were required.

On this large station, owning over 100,000 sheep, the shearing sheds are six miles from the house, fortunately for my lady friend, who is thus spared all the ceaseless worry of superintending the housing and feeding of the numerous shearers during this busy time.

This favoured spot has the best climate in Queensland, being situated some 1500 feet above the sea-level, and most certainly the best climate I have experienced in the Colonies generally.

Even during my summer visit (March) with a thermometer ranging from 74° to 86° in the shade, the mornings and evenings were generally cool and the heat is dry; not wet and relaxing like Sydney. Perhaps for once the weather was "exceptional" in a favourable sense of the word, and doubtless the heat is greater in January than March; but the "Darling Downs" must be considered superior to any other part of the

district, for the nearest market town of Toowoomba is quite a
sanatorium for the poor sun-scorched sufferers on the plains
where Brisbane is situated, at a distance of only seven hours
by train from Eton Vale.

This vale is an extensive stretch of smiling and lovely
country, surrounded by "green hills, far away," with fine
pasturage of lucerne, "blue grass," &c., &c., and has the very
loveliest clouds and sunsets that I have seen away from Egypt
and California.

My stay had been prolonged owing to the delay in the
start of the China Navigation Company's ship *Changsha,*
in which my friend and I had taken passages for Hong Kong,
and which was sent into quarantine on her arrival from China
owing to the usual outbreak of small-pox on board. This, I
believe, is an almost constant occurrence when ships come
from the Celestial Country. However, all pleasant things
have an end, and only too soon I found myself in the train
for Brisbane, where we arrived at ten o'clock one night, after
a wearisome seven hours' journey.

Brisbane is a bright, pretty, clean-looking city, with some
fine buildings, some lovely Botanical Gardens, and one of the
most beautiful drives in the world, up " One Tree Hill."

Of course we saw all these before starting the last day of
March for Hong Kong. All large steamers touching at
Brisbane anchor in Moreton Bay, several miles from the
city. This gave us the chance of seeing the pretty scenery
of the River Brisbane *en route,* but as some influential

passengers on board the tender insisted on being landed for
an hour or two half-way, we only reached the *Changsha*
at 2 P.M., almost famished, having left our homes at 7.30 A.M.,
and of course without any notion that food would be required
for such a short trip.

However, we found an excellent lunch on board, and I
have never experienced greater comfort on board any steamer
than was our lucky experience on this China Navigation line.

I had been strongly warned against it, as an " *unknown line
and sure to be beastly,*" by many of those who pin their faith
to the P. and O., and can imagine no comfort or convenience
outside of that time-honoured Company's ships. I can only
repeat that I have *never* met with so much kindness, comfort,
and cleanliness on board any ship as the *Changsha.*

The crew and stewards are all "China boys," quick and
attentive. The food is excellent, and the cabin accommodation
has been planned for human beings, not for pigs, as one
might imagine in going over some of the popular steamers of
more famous lines.

We were very fortunate also in our captain, who treated
us more like guests than passengers, begging that " we would
ask for *anything* we wanted at any time, and it would be
brought to us if practicable."

There was no stewardess on board, but her services were
barely required, for after a day and a half of rough weather,
we got into calm seas, and floated along day after day on a
sea of glass—most ideal from a bad sailor's point of view.

There is only one drawback to this delightful voyage from Brisbane to Hong Kong—namely, the tropical heat which one must endure for the greater part of the three weeks' voyage.

We touched at Townsville and Cookville, and in seven days reached Thursday Island, a very pretty place, where we landed and made great bargains for the large and beautiful oyster-shells with iridescent gold rims for which this island is celebrated, the pearl fishery being carried on here to a large extent. After this, the heat became daily greater, reaching 100° in our cabins, at which point I "struck," and slept in a hammock on deck. The culminating point of our sufferings through heat was reached after passing through the Gulf of Carpentaria and anchoring at Port Darwin, where we were obliged to stay for two days, discharging and taking in cargo.

Mattresses were placed for us all on the upper deck, where we lay side by side—a curious medley of husbands, wives, spinsters, and bachelors. The first night was a brilliant success, but on the second night of our stay, a heavy storm of rain came on quite suddenly about 2 A.M. No one liked to make the first move, as we all felt a little shaky on the score of "costume," but the drenching rain soon settled matters, and in two minutes we were all flying down the companion ladder, dragging our bedding after us as best we might.

Port Darwin lies on a low, flat bit of the coast of *South Australia*, as it is rather absurdly called.

There is a good pier, and the township (Palmerston) has

some pretty, low Government buildings. The town is more Chinese than European, and is very quaint and original, with a broad main road, lined on either side by Chinese and Japanese shops and buildings.

Our afternoons were spent on the veranda of the Governor's house, where a little cool breeze was sometimes to be found—a great boon with the thermometer at 105° in the shade.

On again through the Torres Straits, and in five days we had once more "crossed the line" and returned to the northern hemisphere.

It seemed quite like "coming home again" after eight months in the south.

Passing the Sulla Islands, and later, to our left, Basilan (thirty miles in length, with a town plainly visible called Port Isabella), we came upon the most southerly point of the Philippines—Spanish settlements with a population in all of seven millions.

These islands are well wooded, and looked very fertile and lovely, possessing the additional attraction of insuring us smooth waters, for we were land-sheltered during more than twenty-four hours spent in passing through them.

Even the China Sea treated us well on this occasion, and I felt quite grieved to be leaving the dear old ship, when at last, "twenty-two days out," we sighted the beautiful approach to the harbour of Hong Kong. Many of us thought

I

this harbour even more beautiful than Sydney Harbour, because the colouring is so much more varied. The surrounding hills are high, and rather bare of vegetation, but this is fully atoned for by the rich deep reds and browns of the colouring of the soil, where patches of the grass have been cut up.

The passage at one point is very narrow, just before turning the corner, whence to the left lies the island of Hong Kong, upon which the town (Victoria) is situated.

Numerous Chinese junks were in harbour as we steamed in; ramshackle-looking wooden boats with sails made of matting and bamboo ribs—very heavy and uncouth, and difficult to reef, one would imagine.

A little steam launch belonging to the Hong Kong Hotel took ourselves and our baggage to the wharf, about a mile and a quarter from the ship, and thence a few moments' walk brought us to the hotel, a very fine one, all inlaid with encaustic tiles.

But, oh the heat! Damp, enervating, oppressive, depressing. Hong Kong is said to have a perfect climate during three months of the year—namely, December, January, and February. April is early for such heat as we experienced, but the summer had come on suddenly, taking every one by surprise, and there had been no time even to put up the punkahs, which had been so great an alleviation to our sufferings on the *Changsha*.

Despite the overpowering heat, we took "chairs" on the

first afternoon of our arrival, to see something of the beauties of Hong Kong.

These chairs, made of bamboo, are slung upon very long poles, which rest on the shoulders of one man at each end.

A very heavy person, however, requires three or even four coolies to carry his chair, especially up the steep hills of this city. The jinricksha is also to be found here, and is a much pleasanter kind of conveyance ; for a *chaise à porteurs* always conveys the impression that one is turning one's fellow creatures into beasts of burden. The jinricksha is also drawn by one or more coolies, who run between the wooden shafts; but the effort appears far less than with the chair. The former, however, is quite useless except on fairly level roads, and on this account has never become general in Hong Kong.

We stopped first at the beautiful gardens overlooking the harbour, where Parsees, Hindoos, Chinese, and Japanese were strolling about in their picturesque costumes; many of the men acting as kindly nurses to the puny white-faced European children. Then we paid a visit to the English cathedral, a bare, barn-like building, only relieved by a little good painted glass, but picturesquely situated on high ground amidst the luxurious green of the steep winding lanes that run up from the sea to form the romantic town of Victoria.

Wishing to make sure of seeing Canton, we decided to go on there next day, and I made inquiries from one of the partners of a well-known house to which I had brought letters, as to the possibility of accommodation there, as we wished to spend at least two days in the place. He enlightened my ignorance by announcing that there was no accommodation for visitors. They must either spend only a few hours in the town, transferring to a return steamer in the evening, or, if more fortunate, accept the hospitality of some one of the European merchants or officials who live upon the delightful island of Charmine. We were fortunate in having an introduction to a most hospitable German gentleman who has an ideal house there, where we spent two very delightful days.

Canton lies about eighty miles to the north of Hong Kong, and we went on board the steamer *Fat Shan* about four o'clock one hot afternoon. These river steamers are magnificent in their appointments, the cabins are airy and well furnished, and the *cuisine* would do credit to any French *chef*.

The scenery going out of the harbour was beautiful, and when the moon came up we sat on deck watching the low banks of the river (Hong, or Pearl), and feeling very peaceful and cool after the great heat of the city.

At ten o'clock the steamer anchored for the night, continuing its journey at daybreak, when I peeped out of our cabin window (for these steamers have real windows) and felt much excited by a sight of our first Chinese pagoda. We passed quite close to two of these on the river's bank before reaching Canton, one 170 feet, and the other 200 feet, in height. Every one is familiar with the shape of these pagodas, built in tiers of seven to nine stories, surrounded by verandas of wood painted deep red, black, or white, and with bells hanging round each corner of every tier.

Shrubs were growing out from the verandas, the seeds having been dropped by passing birds.

These are religious monuments, and are supposed to bring good luck to the neighbourhood in which they have been raised, as they are generally dedicated to the god of agriculture, showing that the Chinese have a great idea of the main chance even in their religious observances. One of the pagodas we passed was 600 years old, and the other about half that age.

The greater portion of the native population of Canton live upon the river, in tumble-down old-house boats, many of which are permanently moored along the river-side.

In this way, they escape ground rent, although a small tariff is exacted for river dues. Others have built themselves small wooden huts which are supported upon high wooden piles above the water-level. In these cases, I suppose a boat might be kept by a whole terrace, and "jobbed" for purposes of transit.

Of all miserable, filthy towns—of all ramshackle, tumble-down, desolate-looking holes for houses—I think Canton could give long odds to any other corner of the earth.

Our kind friends, having been warned of our arrival, sent down a young friend to meet us, and we soon found "chairs," coolies, and guide; the latter having a long grey pigtail, and his own chair and bearers!

You pay here at the rate of 50 cents a day to each bearer, three of these being required for each chair. One stout gentleman of our party was obliged to take on a fourth coolie, as his three struck work very soon after our start.

The dollar in China and Japan is only worth three shillings instead of four, so that locomotion after all is very cheap in both countries.

We went all through the bazaars, which appear to stretch out for endless miles of narrow, smelling lanes, and are much like those of Cairo and Constantinople, only far more dirty, and with less tempting wares displayed outside.

To buy the beautiful silks, embroideries, and *crêpes*, which are best obtained here, it is necessary to dive patiently into the very recesses of these "stores," which offer no tempting wares to the passing traveller. Dead cats and dogs hang up here as rabbits and hares would in a poulterer's shop. They are highly glazed, and to be found side by side with sucking-pigs, ducks, and chickens. We also saw the "weavers' quarter," where silk-weaving goes on in looms, very much likeour own in structure.

The bazaars of Canton are stone-paved, very narrow, very noisy, and very nasty.

Some of the Chinese seemed intensely interested in us; others barely moved their heads as we passed. On we went, grasping our "camphor bags" firmly in our hands, and at

length emerged before a Chinese temple called " The Flowery
Forest Temple," where there are five hundred brazen images
representing " Genii," and three very beautiful colossal
figures of the seated Buddha, most peaceful in expression,
and reminding one forcibly of the gigantic Osiris figures in
the Temple of Aboo Simbel in Upper Egypt. Large open
courts lead to these Chinese temples, which are built of wood,
the roofs being covered with porcelain-coloured tubing by way
of ornament, and supported by heavy wooden beams inside.

We ascended later the steep wooden steps of the " Five-
Story Pagoda," getting some weak tea and a splendid view
over Canton from the top veranda.

Each floor of this pagoda is a large oblong room of painted
red wood. Canton is a much larger city than Hong Kong,
the population being about a million and a half as compared
with the 500,000 of the latter place.

On one hill we noticed a large cemetery.

The graves are very quaint. The earth is dug out in the
form of a Moorish arch over the grave, and then faced with
stone ; the more important graves having two or three of
such arches, one within the other.

Many of these stone facings are of granite, others of deep
red sandstone.

Later in the day, we took a *sampan*, a boat shaped like
a diminutive " house-boat," which was most cleverly punted
by one woman, whilst a second rowed at the stern with an
oar fixed by a rope to the boat. The woman in front was a

perfect marvel of strength and skill. She brought us
triumphantly through an apparently hopeless labyrinth of
junks and boats of every description ; pushed off from one,
clung on to another, and managed to steer past all in a most
miraculous manner.   Once or twice, the blocks seemed hopeless ; as much so as the narrowest part of Bond Street in the
height of the London season, and the heat during these long
pauses was overpowering ; but patience won the day, and at
length we arrived at some steps across the river, landed, and
then walked to the house of a Chinese gentleman named
"Ho-qhat," who is always ready to welcome foreigners, and
was personally known to our host.   He lives in a large,
handsome house, the rooms all built in detached sections and
in open court fashion.   We passed from one to another
through stone-paved courts, the rooms themselves showing
picturesque interiors full of *objets d'art* and priceless
carvings in wood and ivory, but spoilt now and again
by some hideous European chandelier or other modern
monstrosity.

Two sons were presented to us—one smiling and amiable,
the other very much the reverse.   The latter refused to
shake hands, and "would have none of us."   The father
tried to atone by extra civility and attention.   A hideous old
man was sent off with the ladies of the party to see a
heterogeneous collection of wives, nurses, and small children
in the "woman's quarter."

All of these were sitting or standing together in one large

room. A grey-headed old lady, busy with some exquisitely fine gold thread embroidery, was Mrs. Ho-qhat senior, and appeared very kind and friendly, although conversation was of course confined to signs.

She and the other wives showed the terribly deformed feet typical of female China, measuring from three to four inches in length. These are firmly bound up so that the extra flesh bulges out from above, making the ankle look like a horse's hock.

How the women can walk is a marvel, but they *do* walk, for one of them had come down to our steamer in the morning, and she managed to get on board without a catastrophe, but of course by help of a stick.

A man of any social standing out here is obliged to marry a woman with small feet for his *first* wife. He may please himself the second time. Some say that the absence of small feet in China is not considered respectable, as women of a certain class here always leave their feet in a natural state, and may be known thereby. I trust, however, that the hideous fashion is dying out by degrees, for we passed many women who were not deformed in this way, and they cannot all belong to a disreputable class.

In the outer courtyard belonging to this house is a sort of memorial chapel, the walls being covered with tablets inscribed in Chinese characters, in remembrance of deceased members of the Ho-qhat family.

Hence we went on to a grand Buddhist temple, said to be

the finest in Canton, " Ho-nam " by name.   Here we came in
for part of the afternoon service. First a big bell inside
the building, and unpleasantly near our heads, was
rung.   Then came the beating of a big wooden drum, and
finally twelve priests marched solemnly in, shaven and
shorn, and with yellow silk gaberdines over their ordinary
grey costume.

They began at once a series of genuflexions, throwing
themselves on the ground eight or nine times, and then
mumbling out one sentence over and over again with
maddening persistency. It sounded like " Yo-te-fu-num "
repeated *ad nauseam.*

As nothing else seemed likely to occur, we left after this
function had lasted for an hour, and were delighted to return
to our beautiful temporary home.

The women in China do all the hard work, and seem to
be much stronger than the men.   They dress their hair in
elaborate bands and twists, made as stiff as a board with
gum and water. I fear this elaborate *coiffure* is only made
occasionally, for no woman could possibly dress her own hair;
and the small wooden " collars " used as pillows support the
erection at night and keep it in order.

Here, as in Japan, the babies are carried on the back, being
slung by strong red bands crossed over the shoulders, a tiny
foot coming down on each side of the mother's hips. In spite
of this impediment, the latter goes about her work as usual,
never for one moment considering the little living burden

she supports. The baby swings from side to side as the mother punts, or cooks, or rows, and a Chinese baby from earliest infancy becomes literally accustomed to the "ups and downs" of life, in a manner far from pleasant, one would think. Moreover, the strain of the position must be physically harmful, and this no doubt is the reason why the Chinese have their legs so wide apart in later life.

One of the horrors of our Canton visit was to imagine what the state of the river must be with all these families living upon it, and then to see them boiling their rice and other eatables with the water, or dipping a tin cup over the side of the boat, the contents of which were afterwards thrown into the saucepan as gravy!

The heat of Canton was as great as that of Hong Kong had been, although the thermometer was only registering 83° in the shade; but this damp, enervating heat is far more depressing, and more difficult to bear, than a dry heat of 105° in the shade would be elsewhere. The mosquitoes also were rampant, and gave one no chance of a comfortable *siesta.* The most exquisite palms, the most delicious bamboo chairs, the most interesting books—all appeared valueless to us on account of this terrible plague; and although we left our kind host with real regret, it was almost a relief to set out, as Jane Eyre did, searching for at least another *form* of misery.

Of course we did not leave Hong Kong without paying

a visit to the famous Peak, which is as important a feature to the town of Victoria as " the Mountain " is to Montreal.

Many of the European residents live on the steep sides of the Peak and the Gap, high hills at the back of the town, from whence the harbour is spread out as a panorama beneath our feet. The ascent is very steep, and we felt much sympathy with our poor coolies, who toiled along manfully, reaching the top in about an hour from the hotel below.

Ladies living on the Peak, and making the ascent daily, say they become quite hardened, and declare that the coolies do not really feel the fatigue at all, but this I cannot quite believe. There is always a breeze to be had up here, and on the evening of our visit it was almost too chilly for prudent lounging about, so we returned to the Gap—a little lower than the Peak—and found an excellent champagne dinner awaiting us, ordered by kind friends who had come up from the hot city later in the day.

Every one drinks champagne in China. Morning, afternoon, and evening, it is offered to all guests; and even in the hotels there is a curious fashion of making the same charge (25 cents) for any " drink " ordered, whether it be plain soda-water, lemon-squash, sherry-cobbler, or champagne.

We returned to Hong Kong by a longer but far more beautiful road. Unfortunately the moon rose too late for us to see much *en route*. There was a great " strike " amongst our coolies when our hosts told them to take us down by the longer way. They started—then chattered together—then put

down our chairs—repeating this performance more than once.
As darkness had come on, it was anything but pleasant to
be suddenly left in the middle of the road every few minutes.
But one of our party was fortunately an old inhabitant, and
knew how to manage the heathen Chinee.

" *Who says no ? Show me the man who says no !* " he called
out sternly, and the ringleader of the insurrection having
been pointed out, and a sort of Riot Act read over him in
pigeon-English, the others all collapsed ; and he himself being
reduced to order, we were soon hurried down the dark hill
paths at a great pace, passing some very handsome houses
belonging to the chief merchants of the place just before
re-entering the city.

Another day we went out to the Happy Valley, where
the European cemetery is placed. It is situated among lovely
trees, shrubs, and flowers of every description, and close by is
the Zoroastrian burial-place. A circular racecourse fills up
the rest of the Happy Valley, and high rocky hills surround
it. Above is the celebrated aqueduct road, a magnificent
road cut out of the sides of the hills, and winding along the
line of the harbour for several miles.

Making allowance for the great heat, which in summer
must be intolerable, Hong Kong far surpassed my expectations
in beauty of situation and general interest. We had only
taken in China as a means of reaching Japan, so that
everything of interest was so much pure gain to us.

I had formed what turned out to be a very true

conception of Shanghai, as a purely European-looking mercantile town, and we had no intention of making any long stay there, but unfortunately missed the connection by a few hours with the French mail to Japan, and so were forced to remain a week, and then take a Japanese line.

The four days' voyage between Hong Kong and Shanghai was made on board a P. and O. ship, and did not increase my appreciation of that line, which is, I think, much over-rated.

It made its reputation at a time when there was little competition, and seems to be living upon it at present. I heard a man say once of a fashionable London lady who had squeezed herself and her children into a tiny house in an irreproachable quarter of the town, that "Mrs. —— would not mind living in a *wheelbarrow* if only it were drawn up on the fashionable side of the street." So it is with some people as regards steamer accommodation. Let it be once considered *chic* to travel by a certain line, and the most wretched accommodation or inferior food will be cheerfully endured by the votaries of fashion who have the true spirit of martyrdom, only "switched off" the right track.

I know nothing by personal experience of the two or three large new steamers of the P. and O. line, or what their arrangements may be, and only wish to note the fact that other lines at least as safe and certainly as comfortable (*e.g.* the "White Star" and "Messageries Mari-

times ") are often tabooed merely because "you meet all
the best people on board the P. and O." A friend of
mine came home from Australia lately on board the
Victoria, one out of six hundred first-class passengers.
The "Vere de Vere" element can scarcely be very great
amongst such a crowd, and I was told, as a matter of fact,
that it was very conspicuous through absence.

It would be impossible to imagine two cities more unlike
each other than Hong Kong and Shanghai. When the
tender took us off our ship, the *Ancona*, we passed to
our right the junction of the two rivers Yangtse and
Whangpoo, and continued up the latter, upon which is
situated the town of Shanghai. It is thoroughly European
—handsome, thriving, prosperous, and entirely uninteresting, like so many people who might be described by
similar adjectives.

Large blocks of fine stone buildings line the Yangtse
road, which fronts the river.

Here are all the great houses of business—the banks,
agencies, clubs, &c.

Many of the great bankers live with their wives and
families over the bank itself, and "mess" with the clerks,
who are all educated and gentlemanly men.

On the Sunday I went to service in the Cathedral, a
handsome red brick building in the Lombardo-Venetian
style. The seats are of cane and wood, which is cool for
summer, but slope backwards at an uncomfortable angle

for getting out of them gracefully. The sermon was fair; the singing not so bad as it might have been, but quite unworthy of the really fine organ; and the congregation looked prosperous; very handsomely dressed as regards the female portion of it—and gave one the impression of great wealth. The one drive in Shanghai is along a flat, dusty road by the river's side, passing the water-works and also some large glass and paper manufactories, which have been built and allowed to remain useless because the proper ingredients for these manufactures have not yet been found.

It seems a pity not to have thought out this little detail before dabbling in bricks and mortar.

The crops here are of other grains besides rice, and remind one therefore of England.

The grass is in splendid condition, and the crops seem most flourishing. The temperature was quite cool, and a very pleasant contrast to Hong Kong, but we were told that in the height of summer Shanghai is quite as unbearable as the former city.

The jinricksha is much more used here than in Hong Kong owing to the flatness of the roads. It reminded me of a bath-chair with a hood cut short, and supplied with shafts, between which runs the coolie, who draws you at a capital pace.

I found later, in Japan, that with two coolies, on a fairly good road, one could easily calculate upon five miles an hour.

he most grotesque-looking vehicle in Shanghai is a sort of wooden wheelbarrow, which can be hired by the job or by the hour. It is just a flat board with one huge wheel in the middle, and a couple of wooden handles, which are grasped by the man who pushes it along the road.

The wheel rises up through the middle of the board, and is covered by horizontal bars of wood, which divide the barrow intwo. A whole family will go out for an airing in one of these. The mother, baby, and one other child on one side, two or three older children on the other side, and *paterfamilias* pushing the primitive carriage along. The only interesting part of Shanghai is the "native quarter," but a guide and unlimited camphor-bags are necessary to make the expedition, and all "native quarters" belonging to the same nation bear a strong family likeness.

A Chinese orphanage situated about six miles from the city, and established by French Jesuits, interested us very much.

Two or three pleasant-looking French nuns showed us over the large buildings, which are kept in perfect order, and looked very clean and neat.

Some of the inmates are tiny babies, foundlings left at or brought to the doors—others are older.

There is also an infirmary for the old and sick poor, and finally a *pensionnat* for rich young ladies who pay for their education, and show their "caste" by the tiny little feet of the aristocratic Chinese.

K

In China, as in America, I found that the poor "heathen Chinee" has been in some ways much maligned.

Now that the Chinese threaten to overrun the face of the earth, and are being forcibly kept out of the Colonies, as well as America, by heavy capitation fees, it seems impossible for many Europeans to give them credit for *any* good quality.

That they possess some really fine characteristics is evident when one speaks to those who have had the most practical experience of them.

In America I heard several instances of their faithful and often disinterested service from those who had employed them for years.

More than one housekeeper in Sydney told me of their code of honour amongst themselves.

One lady said to me : " If you employ one Chinaman to bring you vegetables you are absolutely free from importunity with regard to any other. Sometimes a stranger will come and ask me to buy his vegetables, but I have only to say, ' *No wantchee*, other John come here,' and the man goes off without a word. They never dream of interfering with each other in this way."

In China, as also later in Japan, every merchant I came across assured me that he would rather do business with a Chinaman than a Jap.

The latter are pleasanter in manner, but the Chinese are more dependable.

One of the best known merchants in Hong Kong said to me upon this head : " Of course a Chinese merchant will drive a bargain when he can, and try to get the best possible price for his tea or other crops; but when the bargain is once struck, and the price agreed upon, you can absolutely rely upon his sending goods up to sample. So much so, that in our houses it is quite unnecessary to overlook the bulk of the tea sent when once the quality and price have been decided."

Possibly a few of our own merchants might take a hint from the despised Chinaman, who is so generally denounced as the curse and scourge of modern civilization.

It may be necessary to keep Chinese labour out of the Colonies, and thus prevent " the dogs " from eating " the children's meat," but it is as well to be honest about it instead of slandering the poor wretches, as is our present fashion.

Many of them are doubtless wicked and corrupt, but this is *not* the true reason for their persecution. Profligacy that spends its money royally and pays its way never gets persecuted, not even by British respectability.

But the Chinese bring down the cost of labour in those countries where it has hitherto fetched an abnormal price.

The Chinese have two grand and cardinal sins in European eyes. They are too industrious and too frugal in their habits. The first enables them to make money, the second prevents the spending of it, and in this way large sums of money find their way out of the country where Chinese labour is still permitted.

It is quite natural to resent these facts and to endeavour to put down Chinese labour and competition, but it is quite unnecessary to excuse such action by falsehoods.

Moreover, it may be very unpatriotic, but I fear till the end of time, masters and mistresses will prefer low wages and civility to high wages and insolence, which is too often the "Irish and colonial mixture" in domestic service.

Chinese labour would have no chance, if it were not for the class who employ it.

Why not put the saddle on the right horse by taxing *them?*

This might hasten a solution of the question. In any case, good will have come out of apparent evil, for the very fact of Chinese competition must have had a salutary effect upon the domestic tyrants of many a distracted householder.

CHAPTER V.

JAPAN.

Shanghai to Japan—The American Minister's wife and daughter—Talks about Pekin—Nagasaki—Temples and tortoiseshell—The inland sea—Kobè—Japanese passports—Japanese art—Arrival at Kioto—A wet welcome—Buddhist and Shinto temples—The two religions—Katsura rapids—Jinricksha torture—Japanese tea—The cataracts—Kimonas and obis—The ubiquitous bamboo—Shinto lanterns—*Cloisonné*—A Japanese theatre—*Chacun à son goût*—A Japanese uideg—Trip to Osaka and Nara—The Osaka mint—An ancient castle—The arsenal—Modern Japan—How I mounted a Japanese pagoda—Beautiful Nara—The sacred deer—First experience of life in a tea-house—Primitive arrangements—No rose without a thorn—Dancing girls in Japanese temples—A colossal Buddha—Tea gardens at Uji—The process of manufacture—More temples—Good-bye to Kioto! —A Japanese lake—A gigantic cedar—Steamer accommodation—Nagoya—A grand old castle—Ancient Japanese art—Fuji-yama—Approach to Yokohama—A Japanese *fête*—A week at Tokio—Imperial household department—An awkward question—The Shiba—Tombs of the Shoguns—Similarity between Buddhism and Roman Catholicism—The Mikado's new Palace—Hora Kiri and the iris—Japanese Christianity and European civilization—A hint for Exeter Hall—Landscape gardening in Japan—A native dance—The Dai Gakko—Japanese universities—A fortunate meeting—A Japanese Kindergarten—The romance of the Ronins—Dying for a sentiment.

HAVING decided to take through tickets from Shanghai to Liverpool, *viâ* Japan, Vancouver, and the Canadian Pacific line, it was an agreeable surprise to find that we could get

them for the moderate sum of £52 10s. Moreover, this gives
you the choice of returning either from Quebec or New York,
and by any line of steamer, with the one exception of the
North German Lloyd.

We sailed from Shanghai to Japan by a boat (the *Satsuma
Maru*) belonging to a Japanese line of steamers. The ship,
however, had been built at Glasgow, and was commanded by
an Irish captain.

The wife and daughter of the American Minister at Pekin
were amongst our fellow-passengers, and the former quite reconciled me to our great disappointment in being forced to
leave Pekin out of our programme. Time and strength had
both failed us, for we should have required ten to fourteen
days for the journey, a great part of which is over terrible
roads, in rough bullock-carts.

The real drawback, however, lies in the fact that there is
comparatively little to be seen on arrival, owing to the strict
seclusion in which the Emperor and Empress live. Even
high foreign officials who have lived in the city for years find
it impossible to break through the "celestial" conditions.
So the ordinary traveller would stand a very poor chance.
The Emperor shuts himself up in his inner or sacred kingdom,
and sees nobody. When he visits the temples orders are sent
beforehand for all foreigners to clear out.

The Empress gives receptions, but is always seated behind
a screen on these occasions, and is not allowed to show
herself.

Mrs. Denvey did, however, receive a visit from the Prince and Princess Koom whilst staying in her country house near Pekin. He is an uncle of the Emperor, and it is quite against rules that these sprigs of royalty should visit foreign ministers, but the Prince had come upon this occasion in order to gratify his wife's urgent wish to see a European for the first time in her life. She took tea with Mrs. Denvey, but had taken the precaution of bringing her own cup and saucer, not being allowed to drink out of any other.

The Yellow Sea is certainly an unpleasant experience; a short "choppy" sea, which good sailors declare is "no sea," but quite enough to settle matters for bad ones.

On the second morning we came to anchor at Nagasaki about 7 A.M., and had our first view of Japan. Nagasaki lies at the head of a pretty harbour, surrounded by hills with trees growing along their very crests, and reminding one irresistibly of the Japanese tea-trays. Several Russian men-of-war were lying in port, and likewise a large Russian convict ship.

After breakfast we took a *sampan* and went on shore being horribly persecuted by the jinricksha drivers, who pursued us on all sides, closing us in from time to time, to the great indignation of an irascible German colonel, who had volunteered his escort. We should have saved much time, temper, and strength by submitting to the inevitable, and choosing out three jinrickshas at once, but the colonel was inflexible, and at last we reached the post-office, worn

out by heat and worry and the distracting shrieks of the Jap
drivers, interspersed with a few good strong German oaths
wrung from our companion in the desperation of the moment.
Here we gave in at length with a very bad grace, and to our
intense relief we were soon being whirled through the bazaars,
and admiring by hasty snatches the pretty lacquer and
tortoiseshell stores, for which Nagasaki is especially famous.

We visited two temples, which seemed very much like
those we had left behind us in China. It is only in Kioto
and gorgeous Nikko that the characteristic Japanese temples
are seen in perfection. Here in Nagasaki we found the
usual gateway of pretty artistic carved wooden roofs filled in
by tiny mosaics of wood. Then came several flights of stone
steps leading into a large square, or oblong courtyard, round
all four sides of which were similar roofed-in buildings. Three
sides of the courtyard are filled by the dwellings of the
priests and officials connected with the temple, the last side
being occupied by the temple itself. In the latter is always
to be found a figure of Buddha, generally flanked by tiny
shrines looking like small cupboards, each with its small
hanging lamp kept constantly burning.

The inner sanctuary can only be approached in what
the Scotch call "your stocking feet," and in Japan no
slippers are provided, as in the Turkish mosques, for the
benefit of sightseers.

Later one became more reconciled to the nuisance of
taking off and putting on one's boots of many buttons several

times during the afternoon, and on many a hot day the relief of walking on the soft straw carpets, unfettered by the hard, unyielding leather, was so great that it became difficult to sympathize with the "poor bare-footed creatures" who have hitherto roused my compassion. The difference between winter and summer must be taken into account, but remembering the exquisite relief of those days, it still seems to me that boots and shoes are doubtful blessings.

Leaving the harbour of Nagasaki, and passing through the beautiful inland sea, too often, as we saw it, enveloped in mist and cloud, two days more brought us into Kobè harbour, where we were to disembark and begin our tour through Japan.

The inland sea was not entirely what Mark Twain would call "a sealed book" to us, but having had a glorious summer's evening when first entering it, on leaving Nagasaki harbour, we were forced to be content later with glimpses of the exquisite islands and mountains, which only served to whet our artistic appetite, and tantalize our artistic senses.

One small glimpse served to show us a celebrated rock, very steep, but rather shelving, from which the missionaries were flung into the sea when they first came over to Japan. A fair, gentle young American girl, sitting by her mother's side, looked critically at the rock, and thence to a higher and far more abrupt descent from a neighbouring crag. "That would have been such a *far better* place to have thrown them down from," she said sweetly, looking quite surprised when a peal of laughter greeted this blood-thirsty remark.

Kobè lies at the bottom of an amphitheatre of pretty green Japanese hills of a peculiar shape so well known to us all from Japanese landscapes, and with the spur and gully formation, already familiar to me in New Zealand. The vegetation upon them is most luxuriant, consisting just now (May) of exquisite roses of varied colouring, and the beautiful, delicate rose- and lilac-tinted wild azalea.

The exploded European notion of passports obtains with great severity in Japan. Moreover, one passport is not sufficient—two or more are required, according to the parts of the country about to be visited, and some of these can only be obtained by application through your consul to headquarters at Tokio, the present native capital of Japan. A local passport, sufficient to take us to Kioto and Osaka, was easily obtained, and having made sure of this, we went on to see the famous Kobè waterfall, up a pretty winding glade, and well worth the stiff climb that leads to it.

Coming down, we stopped at a temple, and leaving our jinrickshas, saw a very curious religious service conducted entirely by women. They were dressed in flowing garments with wide open sleeves, and crowns upon their heads. Most of the women were old and particularly ugly, which probably accounted for their becoming " vestal virgins " in the service of the temple. The temples in Japan are almost invariably approached through booths of toys and sweetmeats, &c., reminding one of a county town fair.

Kobè is disappointing to the newly-arrived traveller, from its thorough European look, for the native portion of the town lies quite at the back, and is completely hidden from the approach to it by sea. We went all through this native part, passing the usual numerous little shops of curios, baskets, lacquer, tortoiseshell, &c., some nice things, and a great deal of rubbish.

I believe that very good purchases may be made in Kobè by the initiated, but such bargains require time and patience, and in Japan, beyond any other country, people must be prepared to pay well for what is really worth buying. The European markets are flooded by the ocean of cheap "Japanese curiosities," which have poured into our countries of late years. Many of these are pretty enough, but they can be bought in Regent Street as well and almost as cheaply as in Japan, and the enormous demand for Japanese goods bringing such severe competition in prices has had a very disastrous effect upon native manufacture. Quantity has taken the place of quality, since Europeans will not, as a rule, pay for the latter when a similar effect can be gained at a quarter or twentieth part of the cost.

"A primrose by the river's brim
A yellow primrose was to him,
And it was nothing more."

To many people unlearned in native art, and not themselves artistic, one Japanese vase of special manufacture, size,
and decoration, is as good as another.   But the initiated, who
can discriminate between mechanical and artistic labour, will
know that even under these given conditions the one article
may be worth £5 or £6, and the other will cost from £200 to
£300.

In Satsuma and Awata ware especially there is the very
widest difference between the work done by the various
artists employed.   In the Awata manufactory near Kioto I
saw a very handsome vase which was bought for £7 by one of
our party, whilst another of similar size and shape, but finer
workmanship, was valued at £150.

I have been shown in England what was considered a very
fine specimen of Satsuma, and should have thought so
myself before my eye became trained in Japan by seeing work
so far superior in quality.

These finest specimens of Japanese art find their way to
England also, and may be picked up by the "collector" here
and there, but he must be prepared to pay a heavy price, with
the certainty that his purchases will only be appreciated
thoroughly by the elect few.

For myself, had I a few hundred pounds to spare, I should
have spent them in getting hold of some of the antique
fittings of the ancient Japanese temples, which can be picked
up occasionally in the less frequented parts of the country. A
gentleman of my acquaintance, who was in Japan when we

were, was making such a collection, especially with a view
to publishing a book on the Buddhist religions of India
and Japan, and his purchases tempted me far more than
all the embroideries and china and lacquer of modern
days.

We left Kobè one fine afternoon about four o'clock, and
reached Kioto, the former capital of Japan, in two and a half
hours by train, passing some very beautiful and fertile country
en route. Everything was novel to us; the clean and yet
romantic-looking little villages, each with its tiny Buddhist
temple, the heavily-thatched roofs of the houses, with bright
green flags growing from the top, the luxuriant crops of rice
standing deep in the water, then further on the crops of
barley, beans, and potatoes. Every inch of ground is carefully
cultivated, and well repays such care and energy.

Arrived at the primitive Kioto station, we took three
'rickshas (one for small baggage), and began what seemed
an endless journey to our hotel. The distance is really about
three miles, but on that cold and rainy evening, racing
through endless bazaars, head well bent down, and almost
suffocated behind the hood and aprons of the 'ricksha, and
unable even to speak to each other, the time appeared to us
interminable. It seemed as if the coolies could not have
understood our instructions, and must be carrying us off
vaguely to some far distant bourne of their own imagination;
but at last we left the straggling town behind, and then
the pace slackened, and by painful and slow degrees we

mounted the very high hill (Maruyama), upon which is situated the romantic Ya-ami hotel.

Kioto is a large straggling town, built right up a valley, flanked by beautiful hills on either side. It was the capital of Japan, and the residence of the Mikado from A.D. 793 until after the civil war of twenty years ago. The list of Buddhist and Shinto temples to be seen here appears at first over-whelming, but we managed by degrees to eliminate all that had not some special characteristic of building, colouring, or situation, and managed to see a good deal in homœopathic doses.

Sightseeing in Japan is very tiring, owing to the immense distances between the various temples. Where the cities themselves often stretch from seven to ten miles, it can be easily understood that a morning's work may cover a con-siderable area. It would be useless and wearisome to enumerate the many temples we visited. Most of them are much alike, but the graceful lines of the buildings, the amount of space they cover, and the beautiful and varied trees growing around them, make the Japanese temples truly "a thing of beauty and a joy for ever."

A traveller's first attempt in Japan is to distinguish be-tween the Buddhist and the Shinto temples. The outward symbols, as well as the inward faiths, have become so mingled with one another that it is almost impossible to find specimens of "pure Buddhist" or "pure Shinto," whilst any attempt to understand the difference of creed seems to land one in a hopeless maze. Of course I am here referring to ordinary mortals, not to such men as the friend I have mentioned, or Mr. Rhys Davids, either of whom could no doubt give me the most accurate information on the subject. I had the pleasure of meeting the latter gentleman once at a hydropathic establishment, where I remember he delivered a most eloquent speech on my behalf as counsel in a " breach of promise case," but having thus frittered away the time that might have been spent in penetrating the mysteries of Buddhism and Shintoism, I had, in these later years, to puzzle the matter out for myself, and can only give my readers the crude conclusions at which I finally arrived.

Shinto—" the way of the gods "—was the original faith in Japan before Buddhism was imported from India and China. It seems to have been more of a philosophy than a religion, as we understand the latter word. The Shinto temples are much plainer than those dedicated to Buddha. They may be distinguished in various ways—by the peculiar curve of the transverse beams of the wooden gateway (*torii*), through which the temple courts are entered—by the rows of stone or iron lanterns leading up to the principal shrine, and last, not least, by the circular steel mirror which is invariably found in every Shinto temple, symbolizing the self-knowledge (the soul's reflection) which formed the coping stone of the Shinto philosophy. They do not appear to have had any belief in a future state, or the immortality of the soul, although divine honours are paid by them to the spirits of famous princes, heroes, and scholars. In fact Shintoism seems to bear a strong family likeness to a creed that has sprung up of late years in London, whose votaries have christened themselves "humanitarians." Truly there is nothing new under the sun.

The Shinto priests are allowed to marry and to wear their hair long, and can hence be easily distinguished from the close-shaven Buddhist priest. The Shinto temples are usually built upon commanding situations and surrounded by groves of trees, but it is very rare to find a Shinto temple nowadays entirely free from the colouring and ornamentation which mark the Buddhist place of worship.

There has been so much talk of late days of "Modern Buddhism," thanks to Mr. Sinnett and his followers, that every one has some smattering of this creed, and some idea of the principal doctrines involved in its adoption, so that it is needless to enter into the subject. Roughly speaking, it may be said that the Japanese peasantry are rather Shintoist than Buddhist, the dwellers in towns rather Buddhist than Shintoist, as may be demonstrated by the immense number of Buddhist temples in all large towns. The thinking and reading classes are generally "indifferentists," or what we might call agnostics.

In one of the Kioto temples (Sangio Sanguendo, A.D. 1150) I noticed one thousand bronze images side by side. They appeared to be representations of a kind of female Buddha, each with sixteen pairs of hands coming out from either side, whilst a pair of smaller hands was folded across the body of the idol. All these side hands bore various symbols, some looking very much like the Egyptian crook of Osiris, others resembling the "Tau"—the sign of life eternal. Is this female Buddha the ground for Laurence Oliphant's belief in the "Divine Femininity"?

Near this same temple we visited a shrine where the Dai Butzi (or great Buddha) is seen; a colossal wooden figure, merely interesting as showing the materialistic view of a crude nation who considered size and power as synonymous.

As a little relief to the endless subject of Japanese temples, I will here describe a delightful expedition which my friend and I made to the "Katsura" rapids, in the neighbourhood of Kioto. A glorious drive of fifteen miles, through splendid mountain scenery covered with brilliant green vegetation of every hue and shade, brought us to a place called Tamba, where we were to take a boat and shoot the rapids. Trees of wild acacia—pink, white, and crimson—lined our road, whilst trails of the lovely wild wistaria met us at every turn. It required all this beauty to make up for the terrible "back-aching" torture of the jinrickshas. Common humanity seemed to make any "leaning back" a dream of impossible bliss, but I found later that we need have had no scruple on this head— in fact the coolies seem to prefer that one should adopt that position, so I conclude it must regulate the balance of the carriage more favourably for them.

L

We stopped half way at a "tea-house," and were glad
enough to get the little cups of Japanese tea, without milk
or sugar, which are invariably handed round on every
possible occasion. I had tasted it in the "Japanese Village"
in London, and thought it exceedingly nasty, but habit
goes for much, and fatigue for more. This green Japanese
tea, poured out of a baby tea-pot, which is constantly re-
plenished, must be strong, for it is undoubtedly very
reviving.

At Tamba we found some benches and tables roofed over
with bamboo, and here we ate our luncheon, the hostess
providing pretty little Japanese cups for the salt, mustard,
and butter. We had brought ample food for ourselves and
the four coolies, and after a short rest made our bargain
with the boatman for three *yen* (a *yen*, or dollar, is three
shillings here, as in China), and prepared to shoot the
rapids, the carriages being packed into the boat, and the
coolies huddling themselves into a corner to get out of the
way of the three or four men required for the voyage.
The wooden boat (made from the trunk of a tree) was
extremely light, but looked rather clumsy, owing to its
great length—this is necessary, to give plenty of room for
the men to pass to and fro in punting and keeping her off
the rocks. The greatest skill is required, and the expedition
might be a dangerous one with less experienced boatmen.

We passed twenty-four or twenty-five rapids, and there is
always a certain pleasure in the "swirl" of a rapid as you

pass over it, but on the whole the performance seemed to me a very mild one after an experience of Egyptian cataracts. The scenery, however, left nothing to be desired. High hills rose up on either side covered with trails of exquisite wild flowers and flowering shrubs. The sun was intensely hot, and so far as comfort went our seat on the narrow board across the boat was a case of out of the frying-pan into the fire, compared with the jinricksha experience.

We passed various long serpent-like rafts, ingeniously constructed by making holes through the ends of trees and splicing these latter together with strong whisps of bark. Towards the last we came upon a perfect labyrinth of these rafts, some arrived at their destination, others being equipped to be towed along up-stream to our starting point. Very young boys are employed in this towing business—no easy work on these hilly, rocky river sides, where they must skip from point to point like young goats, firmly clinging on to the towing-ropes, which are very fine, each raft being provided with three of them.

Arrived at our bourne (Arishiyama) we landed with our 'rickshas and paid the stipulated price. The boatman, I grieve to say, tried to make it *yen* five instead of three (our first experience of anything like extortion) but he "kotooed" as gaily as ever when he found that we were not to be imposed on.

The Japanese are the happiest and most smiling people in the world, having always a joke and a kindly word for one another. It is the land of poetry, but a poetry that is absolutely practical. They do not seem ever to dream of future possibilities. Present life is a paradise, and a paradise of such easy attainment. A few cents—a little rice for their *chow*—a little tea—*et voilà tout!*

Certainly clothing is no great trouble or anxiety. Men and women alike wear a sort of loose dressing-gown as an outer garment. The most highly-dressed man may wear a sort of jersey and pair of trousers underneath this, but many dispense with both these articles, wearing only a loin-cloth under the *kimona*. Others again of the poorest class wear nothing but the loin-cloth, and seem just as happy and comfortable as the rest. The women have tight-fitting trousers and a gaily-coloured petticoat under the sombre dark blue or dark brown *kimona*.

A man fastens his *kimona* with a plain silk sash passed twice round the body, and tucked in at the back. The *obi*, or girdle of the Japanese women, is far more intricate, and generally brighter in colouring. It is nearly four yards in length and about fourteen inches wide, and is often beautifully embroidered in fine silks. Some of these *obis* are very costly, having been bought for sums varying from £2 to £10 each by comparatively poor women. They are then only worn on state occasions, and handed down as heir-looms in the family, a more modest sash replacing them for ordinary wear.

To arrange an *obi* properly is a very complicated

business to the uninitiated, and the women themselves take some time over the performance, which differs slightly in different hands, but the result is much the same, a sort of square puff at the back, which takes off the very straight look of the dress, and is a pleasant relief to the narrow and somewhat skimpy-looking skirt of the female *kimona*.

The hideous fashion of blackening the teeth after marriage seems fortunately to be going out very much amongst Japanese women, especially in the more civilized parts of the country, but here in Kioto it still obtains to a great extent. It gives a most hideous expression to the face, but I suppose was originally intended to keep a woman faithful to her husband, through absence of temptation.

The most characteristic tree in Japan, as in China, is the bamboo. It is also the most useful. Drain-pipes are invariably made of bamboo. Houses are constructed with bamboo interlaced, and mud filling up the interstices. Carrying-poles are also made of bamboo, to say nothing of the chairs, tables, baskets, matting, &c., made of split bamboo.

The elaborate coiffeur of the Japanese women is too well known to need any description. Their hair is almost invariably black, and generally thick and long. It is smeared with gum before being dressed, which gives to the "bows" of hair the remarkably stiff look they bear. It is the rarest thing in the world to see a "rough" head of hair such as is common in Europe. As the poorest woman requires the services of a "tire-woman" for this style of hair-dressing, one has an unpleasant conviction that the performance must be a rare one.

Another afternoon in Kioto we visited the temple of Kyomizu, which stands on a fine hill, commanding a grand view of the country. It is quite a pilgrimage up the steep stony road that leads to the temple, lined on both sides with booths containing coarse pottery, toys, and rubbish generally, such as you might see in a third-class seaside bazaar in England. The temple is very imposing in situation, but rather of the "rag-bag" description inside, full of tinsel and old gaudy pictures, ribbons, &c.—painted or tied up as votive offerings by the faithful, in memory of benefits received, or in hopes of receiving them for the future.

In one part we saw over a hundred clumsy figures of children, with innumerable frills of coloured cloth round their necks. When a baby or child in a family is ill, a frill is added to one of these dummies, and "then the child gets well again!"

One notices that many of the stone lanterns and small stone pagodas outside the temples are quite choked up with stones and pebbles—another superstition.

"You throw stone—if him stick, that's good—if him fall down, that's bad." This was the lucid description of our guide. I suppose most of us have done equally foolish things in our day, but as an acknowledged custom, of course we exclaimed, as the rest of the world would do, "How very childish!"

A fine avenue of bamboo trees leads from this curious temple to the ancient one of Nishi Otani, the site of which dates as far back as A.D. 290. It was reconstructed in A.D. 1709, and is built in excellent taste in natural cedar-wood. The flowers, birds, &c., which ornament the walls are all carved in this wood, whilst the gates and panels are of dull gold, and large chests of carved wood inlaid with brass handsomely worked fill up the various recesses. The only two colours touched are gold and cedar, and the effect is very striking and harmonious.

Having already mentioned the Awata ware, I need not say much of our visit to the celebrated *cloisonné* manufactory near Kioto, but some of my readers may be ignorant of the tedious process by which it is made. The vases, &c., are of copper—upon this the design is traced with the very finest copper-wire fixed on in the shape of flowers, leaves, &c.—which thus stand out slightly from the vase or other article of manufacture. Then the spaces inside the pattern are filled in by pin points of various colouring matter, and so prepared for burning and varnishing. Some of the work done is terribly fine, most trying to the eyes, and of necessity extremely slow. If wages in Japan were not so cheap (from 8s. a week downwards) it would be impossible to sell these wares even at the high prices they command already.

The most striking illustration of difference of taste lies in my experience of a Japanese theatre compared with that of friends I have met in this country. Several ladies in Yokohama assured me they could not have a greater treat than to spend eight or ten hours in one of these native theatres, unable to understand a word of the language, and simply watching the slow process of some historical drama or tragedy dating back many hundreds of years. I made two or three attempts to correct my own impressions, feeling sure that these latter, not the actors, must be at fault, but I am bound to confess that of all dreary, draughty, miserable ways of spending an evening, a Japanese theatre still appears to me the most detestable.

I will describe one, which will do for all. There is first a low amphitheatre, with gallery running all round it of plain unvarnished wood. The dress-circle or boxes are divided, by about three inches of wood, into squares, and the wooden bench, without a back, is the amount of accommodation to be found in each of these. Those who cannot find room on the bench squat down on the ground, and certainly had the best of it "in our box," for the draught at the back was enough to turn a mill round. This was caused by a series of ventilators carved into the wooden partition behind us.

The play was a most dreary, mystical one, dating back one thousand years. First came up a knight, leading a wonderful horse, made in pantomime fashion, by two men covered with a horse's skin, who pranced and curvetted about in a very realistic way. As the actors usually enter from the front instead of the back of the stage, and walk right through the audience before arriving at this point, one has plenty of time to criticize their clothing and gestures beforehand, and there is no shock of surprise given by an unexpected entrance at any critical moment. We had next the usual big giant; in this case "a devil" to be killed and conquered. Such a "poor devil" as he was, too, so far as any fighting power went! That he should get the worst of it was a foregone physical conclusion, putting any sense of morality out of court.

The ancient Japanese court costumes were faithfully copied, and these were really interesting, especially the long skirts and trousers, lying for several feet upon the ground, which were manipulated with much ingenuity. In one particular the Japanese theatre is certainly an improvement on the Chinese one, namely, that it is much quieter. There is no shrieking or screaming, only the everlasting clapping of two pieces of wood against each other, equally distracting to actors and audience, one would imagine.

A guide is an absolute necessity of travel in Japan when one goes beyond the larger cities, such as Kioto, Tokio, and Yokohama. He must be not only guide, but cook and housemaid as well, for no food is to be found in a Japanese tea-house beyond the usual cup of green tea, and no accommodation with the exception of a few down quilts, which are dragged into your room and there left to be arranged as a

bed by your guide.   Sheets, pillow-cases, napkins, &c., must
all be taken by the traveller, in addition to the pots and pans
necessary for cooking his food, so that travelling in the country
necessitates a fair amount of impedimenta, however modest
one's personal luggage may be.

Travellers will do well to leave all heavy luggage at various
starting points, such as Kobè and Yokohama, and make these
expeditions in the very lightest possible marching order. The
flat Japanese rush baskets, which expand and contract according to the amount packed, are by far the best for this sort of
travelling.   They can be had in every size, but I should
recommend two medium-sized rather than one large one, as
the former pack better in small spaces. As these baskets can
be bought in any Japanese town, and for a few pence, no one
need grudge the expense, even if they are thrown away in a
few weeks.

Intending to make a four days' trip from Kioto to Osaka
and Nara, we made inquiries for a guide, and were fortunate
in finding a nice little fellow, Ya-ami-moto by name, who
wore European dress and glasses, and looked like a very
diminutive foreign student. His charges were, as is usual,
one yen and a half (4s. 6d.) a day, we paying his travelling
expenses, and he finding his own food. He turned out to be
a real treasure, and a capital cook as well.

As Osaka boasts a very fair hotel, we arranged to take
provisions, linen, &c., on from there, as it could be returned
by the coolies, who would bring us back to Kioto viâ Nara.

Osaka lies on the railroad between Kioto and Kobè, and is one of the most interesting towns of modern Japan, being also one of the largest military stations in the country. As Kioto is a reminiscence of old Japan, so Osaka represents the thriving, mercantile, advanced new Japan, which is making such gigantic strides towards modern civilization. This city has a population of 300,000, and its present prosperity and busy life date only some eighteen years back, when the first railway was opened.

Our first visit was paid to the mint. Curiously enough I had never been over one before, so the interest in my case was not merely local. It was quite fascinating to watch the bars of silver and copper taken red from the furnace, beaten out, and put through the machines for cutting dollars and cent pieces as a cook cuts her biscuits with a tin "shape." Another machine stamps these from below and above simultaneously, by a single pressure. The coins are counted out of large baskets full of every kind by an ingenious method, which is probably used in every other mint. A square piece of wood, with slightly raised rounds of the size of each special coin, is dipped into the basket and the coins put in place by a quick movement of the hands. When correctly filled up the board counted out fifty coins at a time.

Other men were engaged in "passing" the coins when first cut (before stamping) to see that they are without flaw, and finally, there is a most ingenious little instrument for weighing the coin when completely finished, to see that it is up to the standard weight. All coins go into this at the same entrance, where there is a little scale fixed, but lower down there are three divisions. Those that are of full weight fall into one of these, the medium weight into another, and the short weight into the third, tumbling out of those holes so marked into three different receivers. All the machinery used in the Osaka mint comes from Paris or England. There are five hundred and fifty men employed in the building, all of them being Japanese.

There is a fine old castle, or rather grand old castle walls, still remaining in Osaka. It is now only a relic of the past, none of the original building being left, but the walls are most imposing. They remain absolutely intact, sloping down to the steep banks of a wide moat, and are said to be more than seven hundred and fifty years old.

All around them are at intervals placed the graceful Japanese minaret houses, which add so much to the general effect of the sweeping lines of the massive grey stone walls. The moat is generally filled with water, but was rather dry at the time of our visit. We climbed up grassy knolls and successions of stone steps inside the huge space inclosed by the walls, and resting on the top of the latter looked down on the panorama of Osaka at our feet. The lovely distant hills formed an amphitheatre on three sides, the fourth being filled in by the deep blue sea with tiny white sails fluttering upon its breast.

The arsenal behind the castle was our next point. This is

a succession of red brick buildings, occupying a large area of ground, and, like everything else in "New Japan," dating only fifteen years back. All the huge guns are made here, and likewise the ammunition for firing them. In one room nothing but machinery repairs were going on. In another, all the bolts and nuts were made. In another long room the enormous sides for artillery waggons are manufactured. In another the "mounting" of the guns is carried on, and so forth.

I noticed some beautiful little brass cannon, with the latest improvements in the way of altering elevation and "charging" the cannon, &c. One might have been going over the arsenal at Woolwich. All the machinery is European, but the Japanese have bought from any country that could best supply their wants, and in the same building may be seen engines and machinery from Birmingham, Dresden, Paris, and Italy. The arrangements for testing the guns have been made by French workmen, and the different weights and calculations are printed in French on the butts from which the trial guns are fired.

Leaving Osaka for Nara we engaged three 'rickshas with two coolies a-piece, and arranged to pay fifteen shillings for each carriage, on the understanding that we should spend two nights in Nara, and be safely conveyed from there to Kioto, whence the coolies would return to Osaka, taking back with them the linen, &c., which we borrowed from the hotel. Our provisions consisted of beef, ham, chicken, two bottles of

Bass, salt, pepper, butter, coffee, tea, and bread, none of which can be procured in a tea-house.

The coolies, as usual, were strong and willing, and trotted cheerfully along at the rate of five miles an hour. We stopped about six miles from Osaka to see the Buddhist temple of Tennoji (A.D. 600), and the oldest temple in Japan.

I made the ascent of a five-story pagoda, scrambling through trap-doors, and up steep ladders in semi-darkness, until at the very top a slit in a wooden wall leads to the outside veranda. I crawled through this on my face in most undignified fashion, but was amply rewarded by the glorious view of Osaka, and only regretted that my friend had not made the ascent with me. Coming down was by far the worst part of the performance, as each stair is simply a long ladder approached by an open square trap-door, through which you must get on to the ladder backwards as best you may.

It was "nasty" work, and only the feeling that I could not remain on a Japanese pagoda for life nerved me to get down each succeeding story. Our little guide had come with me, but was much too small and fragile to afford anything but moral support, which he gave by saying dismally at each fresh descent, "This is a very dangerous place—you can easily slip here !"

His English was very shaky. I think Japanese, in spite of their many other talents, must be poor linguists, or find special difficulty in learning our language, for I have never found it so hard to understand any other foreigners when they attempt to speak English.

I have a vivid recollection of the many hopeless attempts made years ago in London to keep up conversation with a member of the Japanese Embassy, who is now one of the Mikado's most famous ministers.

That Japan would be curious and interesting I felt sure beforehand, but was quite unprepared for the extreme natural beauties of the country. It has all the charm of Swiss mountain scenery toned down by the softened beauty of Italy. The road from Osaka to Nara is peculiarly interesting. Apart from the beautiful line of hazy, poetical blue mountains, the extraordinary cultivation and fertility of the country between these two places is most remarkable. Fields upon fields of golden-eared rice, feathery rape or colza, barley, &c., line the road. Although at first one misses the English hedges, I think the landscape gains by their absence, as there are here no stiff lines of demarcation.

All is scrupulously tended and cultivated, and one crop never encroaches upon another, but there are no arbitrary divisions. Fields of golden rice wave their pretty heads or ears until they touch upon other fields of younger brothers and sisters, just shooting out of the watery ridges, that gave them birth. Then come the crops of clover, bean, and rape, all growing and blending with the lovely line of far distant blue mountains, the fleecy clouds sailing lazily along over a still bluer sky.

The only drawbacks to our day's enjoyment lay in the number of Buddhist and Shinto temples we felt bound to visit on our way. The latter are the more fatiguing, being built on such high ground, and approached invariably by numerous stone steps. But even the Buddhist temples cover such large areas of ground that one has to walk a considerable distance to get round any one of them.

In addition to my pagoda performance I went over three other temples on this particular occasion, and when Ya-ami suggested a fourth, I felt that if Buddha himself had descended as cicerone, I must have declined the honour of accompanying him!

By 5 p.m. we saw in the distance a beautiful pagoda and a town on the hill-side, and knew that this was our destination, Nara. We passed through the usual endless streets of wooden houses, all so much alike and all so clean, and then emerged into some beautiful park-like grounds with a Shinto *horijei* (or gateway) of red wood, forming an entrance to them. Numbers of beautiful tame deer were playing about in these exquisite grounds.

Right up on the very side of the hill, amidst overhanging trees, we came upon our tea-house for the night, "Musashino," and were enchanted by its beauty. We were taken into a little house standing in the gardens apart from the main building, and containing two large rooms separated by the usual sliding screens. These are made of bamboo, the small squares between the strips of bamboo being filled in by tissue paper. They run in grooves and can be shifted to and fro at pleasure, thus forming a very easy but scarcely satisfactory partition, for of course every sound is plainly audible, and it would be extremely disagreeable for others than members of the same party to occupy adjacent rooms. "Except for the honour and glory of the thing" as the Irishman said, two people might as well occupy the same apartment.

In the rooms of a Japanese tea-house there are no beds, no washing apparatus—no table—no chairs—no looking-glass— no anything!

A matted floor, sliding screens all round, an alcove, and at most a Japanese screen in the room itself form the complete furniture. All the tea-houses have a bath room on the ground floor with a large wooden tub in it as is the custom in China; but for any less thorough washing, a metal bowl and a wooden bucket with wooden pot and handle to it, must suffice. These are placed on the open veranda so that the matting of the room may not get wet, and your ablutions must therefore be conducted in full view of the Japanese men and women who crowd round to observe the manners and customs of "the white devils." Other arrangements are still more primitive or generally conspicuous by their absence, no accommodation of any kind being found in a Japanese room.

Alas! we found that so much beauty and novelty had serious drawbacks. Clean as they look and undoubtedly are in many ways, these tea-houses are infested with fleas, especially during the summer months. No doubt this is owing to the matting and the heavy quilts which are piled up on the floor in the place of a bed. Five or six of these are brought in, four are placed one over the other on the floor —then your own sheets are put on, another heavy quilt forms the counterpane, whilst the last one is rolled up to do duty as a pillow.

Ya-ami got a wonderful dinner together for us on the night of our arrival—excellent soup made from our own meat within an hour of reaching the tea-house—grilled chicken, beef cut in squares and garnished with ham and parsley, and a capital sauce (a novel *réchauffé* far superior to mince) —pancakes and coffee. It shows what can be done even in the most primitive part of the world with a charcoal pan and a willing and clever man at the end of it.

The beautiful Shinto temple we had passed on arrival is crowded up outside with stone lanterns (950 in all) which are lighted once a year when the Festa of the temple takes place. It is called Kasuga, and is dedicated to the god of that name (Spring morning) to whom the beautiful tame deer are held sacred.

Dancing girls are dedicated to this temple and they performed a sacred dance for us next morning, an old priest beating time on the wooden clappers generally used for these services. The two girls, thirteen or fourteen years of age, were dressed in wide-spreading kimonas with sweeping, open sleeves, artificial flowers stuck in their elaborately arranged hair, and the whole face covered over with powder and cosmetic making it look like a mask; for the natural skin was left all round the face at the sides. The eyebrows were completely covered over, the eyes looked like little slits in the mask, and the upper lip was also covered, the lower one being painted with red and a dash of gold. The effect was very weird.

They advanced and retired and "kotooed" and whirled about in various attitudes for ten minutes, and then we were told the performance was ended. The priest chanted in a monotonous voice and clapped on conscientiously to the last.

Nara is quite one of the most beautiful spots in all Japan, and with more food and fewer fleas one might spend a month here with the greatest pleasure.

In the temple of Todaiji we saw the colossal Dai Butsu (Buddha) famous as being the largest in Japan. An enormous circular building contains this bronze statue. The figure is sitting on, or rather emerging from, a mass of enormous bronze lotus leaves. It is fifty-three feet high, the length of the face being sixteen feet, and the width of the nostril alone three feet. A man is said to be able to crawl through the latter. This seems improbable, but is doubtless true. I had no wish to attempt the experiment.

The face is very disappointing, having more the expression of a fat school-boy than the dignified repose usually found with any representation of Buddha. There is a grand bronze bell in this temple, one of the two largest in Japan, measuring thirteen feet six inches in height, by nine feet wide at the bottom.

At the Kodaiji temple in Nara, I met with something that interested me very much. There are many paintings here; some very crude ones, commemorating cures and deliverance from various dangers. It was suggestive to notice in several scenes of shipwreck or other calamities, a figure in the air at the extreme right or left corner, surrounded by a sort of halo, representing Buddha come to the rescue or consolation of the sufferers. Now we know that the Buddhist religion did not take root in Japan until A.D. 600. Were such representations of Buddha indigenous to that religion, or were they introduced as a corruption or legend of Christianity 600 years after the death of the Founder of the Christian religion ?

Returning from Nara to Kioto, we passed Uji, where the great tea-producing industry is carried on, and stayed a few hours to watch the various processes. Many people are familiar with the low, stumpy-looking, close round bushes of a tea plantation, but all may not have watched the operation of tea-making. In the Uji neighbourhood the finer teas are all grown under matting covers overhead, and at the sides of the bush, to preserve it from the too

fierce rays of the sun. It is all green tea here, that is
to say, made from the fresh green leaves.

These are picked and laid on mats to dry. Then they
are "washed" and put in a colander to steam for a few
minutes. They are then turned into large trays over a
hot fire. Men quite naked with the exception of a
loin cloth, next roll the leaves over and over this stove,
and pass them on to an expert, who gives the final rolling,
after all twigs, &c., have been picked off by the women
who do that special work. The tea is then packed away
in huge jars, made air-tight, and is fit for use.

It was well to have this diversion, for the road from
Nara to Kioto is not otherwise interesting, and being bad
and hilly, we were obliged to walk during a large part of
it, and as the rain came on heavily towards sunset, we
were very thankful to arrive at the large straggling town
of Kioto once more. It seemed quite homelike to us, as
we recognised with some triumph the turn to our hotel,
up on its lofty eyrie on the mountain side, and found
ourselves once more in the Ya-ami inn.

Anxious as I am to spare my readers "vain repeti-
tions" with regard to the innumerable temples of Japan,
I must say a few words about the famous Kinka-Kuji
(gold-coloured temple) which lies at the foot of the beautiful Kinkasayama mountains in the neighbourhood of
Kioto.

It is a small wooden temple about five hundred years

old, situated in the midst of lovely gardens, the latter being the real attraction to the place. It was built as a summer residence by the Shogun Yoshimitsu. The Shoguns were formerly the Military Governors of Japan, who shared, and for many years overshadowed the temporal power of the Mikado himself. A little monumental stone on a miniature island in the grounds, is raised in memory of a fabulous white serpent, which is said to have lived here in ancient times. Some steps lead from one elevation of these beautiful gardens to another, until at length a little summer-house is reached, at the very top of all, built like a Japanese tea-house.

Down below a large sheet of water is covered with water-lilies and fringed by beautiful blue iris. In some rooms belonging to a more modern part of the building, are kept various domestic relics of the famous Shogun Yoshimitsu, whilst the walls are lined by some clever spirited black and white paintings done by Kanone, a celebrated Japanese artist who flourished two hundred and eighty years ago, and whose name is still held in the greatest reverence in this country.

Leaving Kioto one morning in brilliant sunshine, after a fortnight's happy stay there, we took our guide Ya-ama-moto, and went by train to Otsu on Lake Biwa, only an hour's journey, but sufficiently interesting to tempt us to stay for a night in order to explore the neighbourhood.

First we drove for some miles along the lake shore to

see a grand cedar, a wonderful specimen of tree training two thousand years old. The top branches had been carried off by a severe storm three years ago, but this is less to be regretted since height is not the most striking feature of the growth. The marvel lies in the immense width of the tree and the stretch of the branches. It measures four hundred and fifty feet round the branches, the diameter being one hundred and fifty feet.

Driving back past Otsu, and for some miles along the other end of the shore, we came to the beautiful village temple and grounds of Ichiyama. Few travellers come here, but it commands one of the most glorious views in Japan. We climbed the usual stone steps, then through lovely wild gardens to a terrace, where we found the inevitable temple and a marvellous view of mountains, lake, and stretches of smiling, cultivated ground at our feet.

Otsu is one of the dirtiest towns we saw in Japan, and the men and women are far less neat here than elsewhere in their dress. Large military barracks are built outside the town here as at Osaka, and I was much puzzled by the difference of size and strength in the soldiers to the ordinary Jap. Some light was thrown on my perplexity when I read Griffith's book on Japan, and found that from generations back the Japanese soldier had represented a special class picked out in the first place for extra size and strength, and so being bred as carefully and surely as dray horses or collie dogs.

Lake Biwa rather disappointed us. The scenery was somewhat tame, and the steamer accommodation far from pleasant. The boat was crowded with Jap who lay about on rugs spread upon bales of cotton, and were far better off than we first-class passengers. Our little guide tried in vain to make us stay down in the first-class cabin, a stuffy place, whence we could get no view of the lake. The deck was supposed to be only for second-class passengers so doubtless he felt his honour at stake should we be seen there by his fellow countrymen.

Fortunately the voyage lasted barely five hours, and then four hours by train brought us to Nagoya, and our quarters for the night. This train had no first-class carriage, and only one long second class, which was quickly filled up by Japs. All the men smoked. Two young Japanese ladies accompanied by two older women, a young man and a boy made up one party, and were as friendly with us as Tower of Babel drawbacks would allow. They were afterwards our fellow travellers in the steamer to Yokohama, but never emerged from their cabins during the short voyage, and did not take part in any European meal on board. One of the young girls had the very prettiest hands I have ever seen, with small white dimpled and pointed fingers, a fit subject for some lucky sculptor.

Nagoya is a flat, clean, uninteresting town but is the fortunate possessor of one of the most famous and beautiful castles in Japan. It reminded us at first sight of the Osaka castle, but whereas the latter is in ruins, the principal portions here remain in the shape of a four or five-storied building situated at one side *on* the walls and not surrounded by them as our castles are. The wooden roofs are all covered over by copper tiling. There are large gloomy corridors, passages, and dormitories in the castle, but it is quite uninhabited nowadays.

Down below are some interesting rooms decorated with pictures, some in colour, others in black and white; also the works of the famous Kanone. The subjects are generally animals, lions, tigers, leopards and birds of every description. They are extremely clever and spirited, quite unlike the flat style of Japanese art which obtains in these modern days. Some of the pictures contain representations of temples and other buildings, in which a wonderful knowledge of perspective was very evident.

Although our guide had gone out at cock-crow to get tickets for the castle, the delay in letting us in was immense. We had to show all our passports several times to different officials, who came out and stared at us and then went away again. A soldier was told off to accompany us, but on these occasions it is not considered etiquette to offer any "fee." No single official in the lowest government capacity will take a penny—a sure proof that the Japs are not yet entirely civilized or Europeanized!

Hurrying off to Miya, the suburb and port of Nagoya we and our modest luggage embarked in the tender which was to take us to our Yokohama steamer, the *Hiroshima Maru*. The Captain of the tender, and eight or nine Japanese sailors were much taken up with looking at our rings, watches and other trinkets at first; but very shortly the tossing and whirling of that horrible little boat even on a fairly calm sea drove me down to the cabin, where I found our poor little guide stretched out in speechless misery.

Three hours brought our sufferings to an end, and feeling very much like a washed-out rag, I clambered up the sides of our fine, larger steamer, belonging to the same line as the one by which we had arrived in Japan.

Next day we spent a peaceful morning on deck, watching through the clouds to our left, the dim snow-tracked outline of the famous "Fuji-yama." The clouds lay too low for us to catch even a partial glimpse of the graceful sweeping lines of the sacred mountain with which we became afterwards so familiar. All the morning, the land view was extremely pretty, culminating at length in the harbour and town of Yokohama which we reached at noon.

There are two rival hotels in Yokohama, the "Club" and the "Grand." We had sent on our heavy baggage to the former, and the hotel man arrived in the steam launch with our letters, and seemed much relieved to have us safe in his charge whilst upon that occasion his less fortunate companion made a fruitless trip.

Yokohama is a purely commercial town, built by Europeans, and is no more interesting in itself than Liverpool or Bristol,

but it is an excellent centre for touring, and many of the
most beautiful and interesting places in Japan are within
a day's journey of the commercial capital. Of course there
is a large native quarter here as elsewhere, and many of
the native shops, especially those in a part called the
Benten Dori, are very tempting. We drove all through
the native town on the evening of our arrival, for there
was a special Festa of some days going on to commemorate
the "first day of summer," which is fixed for the second
day of June. Chinese lanterns hung before every door,
and many marionette shows and other entertainments were
in full swing as we passed.

Most of the Europeans, consuls, barristers and other
officials and wealthy merchants, live upon the Bluff, some
beautiful heights overhanging the harbour and within fifteen
minutes of the esplanade, but approached by a very steep
ascent. The harbour is ever bright and cheerful, for so
many ships from different quarters of the globe lie always
within sight.

Within an hour by train of Yokohama is Tokio, the real
capital of Japan and residence of the Mikado and all the
higher Japanese officials. We spent a week here, and found
something to occupy every moment of our time. The
English Legation is at Tokio, and all passports and government "permissions" must be obtained from thence. A permission to visit some of the principal gardens in Tokio (belonging
to the Mikado) gave us as much pleasure as anything.

Japan is the country *par excellence* for landscape gardening and the "gardens" in Japan are all the more lovely
for having so few flowers.   This sounds a paradox, but the
trees are so beautiful in shape and foliage and the flowering
shrubs so numerous and varied that one never seems to
miss the flowers.   Wild flowers grow in the greatest
profusion, the roses and azaleas so highly cultivated with
us, coming under that head out here, but a real "garden"
in Japan generally means only shady trees and shrubs
and most beautiful they are, mingled with the delightful
grottoes, rockeries and rustic bridges which adorn every
pleasure ground, no matter how small it may be.

Tokio   is   an   immense   city,   situated   near   the   sea
and occupying nine miles in length by eight miles in
breadth.   In 1888 the population had risen to two millions
as compared with one million of inhabitants in the year
1885 !

We had gone to Tokio without a guide, having a great
love of being independent if possible, but we soon found
out our mistake, and remedied it on the following day.
The coolies are very ignorant of English, and it was impossible to make them understand the simplest direction.
After traversing several miles they came suddenly to a
full stop before a building which we had not the slightest
curiosity to investigate at the time.   Later on we found
out that it was the "Imperial Household Department."
In vain we suggested going on—the 'ricksha men were

inexorable, and tried to make us understand by signs that it would be quite easy to gain an entrance.

The civil sentry kept us for more than half an hour whilst he despatched messages to various officials who came out one after the other; all in uniform, and all as helpless as himself. At length one poor man after looking at us in speechless agony and then nearly going off in an apoplectic fit in his effort to frame an English sentence, burst out with it in the form of the following query, *Why do you come here?* Upon my word I did not know how to reply—the question seemed so pertinent. "I have not the vaguest notion, ask the coolies" was the only answer that suggested itself, and I could not put that into Japanese, and I am sure he had exhausted his whole English vocabulary. It ended in our driving off ignominiously, leaving him master of the situation.

Profiting by experience, we took a guide next day to the Shiba, (a grass plot) a sort of inclosed park of pleasure grounds and temples. Foremost of these latter in interest is the Zojoji (Buddhist) temple, where the tombs of the Shoguns are to be seen. It was one of the handsomest temples we had seen, with beautiful carvings in wood, covered with gold, crimson, pink, and cream. The roofs are composed of squares of lacquer with pictures inside, reminding one constantly of the beautiful Italian roofs to be seen in the palazzi of Florence and Venice.

In the uppermost temple are three gorgeous gilt shrines

of the Shoguns, with images of Buddha and Kwanon (god of mercy). The wood in these Japanese temples is stained crimson with sulphate of iron, which is also used for embalming, and is very costly. The tombs of these Shoguns were handsome bronze cupolas, with the arms of the Shogun (three geranium leaves) carved upon them. From the top of these bronze monuments rises a device suggesting in bronze the idea of a flame rising direct from the tomb towards the sky. This is said to be an emblem of the spirit which rises like a flame from the natural body.

"Vital spark of heavenly flame."

Is there anything new under the sun?

The large stone baths of holy water before all the temples are used by worshippers for washing their hands before prayer. To make the sign of the cross with it was only one step further with the early Christians. The Roman Catholics must surely have borrowed all these lamps, shrines, votive offerings, pictures, and holy water, from Buddhism—for what intercourse can the Buddhists have had with them since the Christian era until these latter days?

There are more than two hundred stone lanterns in front of this temple, where again we can note the mixture of Shintoism with pure Buddhism. These lanterns were given to the memory of the deceased Shoguns by their humble retainers. The richer ones gave bronze lanterns, of which some handsome specimens stand in the inner court of the temple.

On our way home we passed the Shiro or castle, and saw the new buildings for the Emperor's palace. Some months ago, permission was easily gained with a little interest, to see the new palace, but being now so near completion, all such privilege was suspended. The old palace was burnt down ten years ago, and the Mikado was occupying temporary quarters last year whilst his new home was being completed. The new buildings are very unpretentious but in good taste, and most harmonious in colour, with a number of brown roofs at various angles. The decorations inside are said to be most beautiful. Fortunately it is thoroughly Japanese in character, and therefore far more beautiful and characteristic than any European building could have been with similar surroundings.

Another day we took an interminable drive to Hora Kiri, one of the sights of Tokio at this time of year (June). It is an excavated ditch turned into a pleasure ground and planted with beds of iris, which grow to great perfection in the water here, showing every lovely shade of mauve, deep blue, faint grey, &c., &c. The blossoms are of immense size as well as beautiful in colouring, and I felt that I had never appreciated the flower before, although it has always been one of my prime favourites.

One becomes so accustomed to the kindliness and friendliness of the Japanese that it is apt to pass unnoticed after the first few weeks. It is however most remarkable, especially the quiet good humour so universal in the streets. All travellers have noticed this, but it seems to come with a fresh shock of surprise to each of us. I have never heard any quarrelling in the streets, nothing approaching to a fight, nor have I ever noticed any unkindness or quarrelling between children, nor any attempt amongst the elder ones to bully those younger or weaker than themselves.

If a child cries in the street from fright or loneliness, some one (generally a man) invariably rushes out from his shop, picks the little one up in his arms and soothes it with loving words and looks. It is the same with the grown-up people. The poorest men are just as scrupulously polite to each other as the grandees of a European court—the same low bows when they meet, hats off, bodies bent and the most courteous and charming smile.

They are a wonderful people truly. I fear that civilization will spoil them—certainly it will sadden them by introducing elements of morbidness and self-analysis into their present simple, happy lives.

I should like to see the faces of some of the very " good " Exeter Hall people if it were suggested that a fund should be raised for sending over Japanese missionaries to England to convert *us!* And yet I am sure we might learn many lessons in Christianity from them in the way of courtesy, kindliness towards each other and cheerfulness of mind.

Differences of taste and opinion are never more apparent than in travelling. Hence it is so impossible to gain by the experience of others unless one knows beforehand and makes due allowance for personal prejudices. For instance, a lady friend in Tokio had strongly advised us to give up an expedition to the private gardens of the Mikado in the Shiro grounds, assuring us there was nothing of any interest or beauty there. I discovered later that her one idea of a garden was a place where *flowers* grew. Now Japanese gardens have comparatively few flowers, and no conventional "flower-beds" such as we cultivate in Europe. Wild flowers, which here include azaleas, wistaria, and iris, &c., as well as roses, grow in beautiful profusion in the gardens as they do on the road-side or amongst the hills, but, as I have said before, trees form the great beauty of a Japanese garden. These are most lovely in foliage and in the varying tints of green on the same tree, and often so immense in height.

Their trees are as gigantic as the Japanese themselves are small. One of the most beautiful Japanese trees, growing sometimes to a considerable height, at others a mere large bush, is the maple. It is quite different from the American maple, for the leaves are of the tiniest dwarf description, even when the tree itself is large. These leaves exhibit every shade of tender green, whilst others are crimson, flame, or copper-coloured, these latter being the natural colour and not autumnal tints, which were still far distant in the month of June.

A Japanese garden is a delicious combination of "wild and tame"—Nature is encouraged, never coerced or tortured. There is no uniformity, no cold regularity to take all the poetry out of a garden as with us. Here you find water

N

everywhere—often artificial, but hiding all sign of art—rockeries, stonework, and beautifully arched but rough stone bridges thrown across the water, undulating grassy hills and stately trees throwing their beautiful shadows everywhere.

Such gardens have all the charm of a forest scene and all the cultivation of a park. Here again we might take a useful lesson from the Japanese. Think of our "tortured" trees and uniform beds of bedding-out plants! I suppose space is one great necessity for such gardening, and this is found more readily in Japan than in England, but if we *had* more room we should only plan out more "conventional" beds, and perhaps train a few more trees into impossible shapes.

Although my experience of "native dances" has proved them to be almost invariably an expensive and wearisome failure, we felt bound to see the *geisha* or "dancing girls" of Japan, so an evening was fixed, and our guide made the necessary arrangements for the exhibition at one of the noted tea-houses. It was a large and handsome house, containing some excellent pictures and some fine specimens of bronze and lacquer work. The flower decorations consisted of a single group of beautiful white arum lilies in one corner of the room.

We squatted down as best we could on low cushions on the matted floor, and presently the dancing girls came in. They were very young, the two eldest being apparently about thirteen or fourteen years of age, and the third a tiny child of seven or eight, who danced the best of the three, and was most amusing in her posturing and self-possession. The "music" consisted of one woman who played a native instrument, a sort of drum shaped like an hour-glass. This was made of lacquered wood, with pig-skin stretched across either end of it, red cords as thick as the little finger stretching lengthways all round it. These strings or cords when tightened or relaxed give varied tones by alternately pulling out and contracting the pig-skin.

The chief point however consists in striking the pig-skin of the instrument very sharply at either end with the flat of the hand. A worrying, wooden sort of sound is the result, by no means pleasing, especially as it was accompanied by shrieks and squalls from the performer, reminding one irresistibly of cats squalling on the top of a wall. Two other women played each an instrument like a square banjo, called a *samisen*; this has three strings, and is played not with the fingers but with an ivory stick. Discordant groans and shrieks accompanied the whole performance.

The dance itself seemed easy enough. Each girl twisted and twirled, and turned round, and postured according to her own sweet will, apparently without any regard to what the others were doing, but I suppose there must have been some method in the madness, for they turned up now and then close to each other with fans all pointed in the same direction. Four or five dances were conducted on similar lines; some in praise of spring, summer, winter, &c.; others

descriptive of the maple, wistaria, and other characteristic
trees and flowers.   Sweetmeats and tea were handed round
at intervals, the former apparently composed of pomatum
and salad-oil with a little crystallized sugar at the top!

Every one visiting Tokio spends a day if possible at Ueno,
a sort of immense pleasure-ground, similar to the Shiba
already mentioned.   Here, in addition to temples and
zoological gardens, we found a large museum—a modern
red-brick building, containing some very handsome rooms,
but a very poor collection so far as European goods are
concerned.   The native collection is very beautiful, especially
of bronzes and lacquer work, but the foreign department is
very inferior, and I fear the poor Japs have been terribly
cheated by those who bought for them, unless the latter were
exceptionally ignorant.   Tawdry artificial flowers, the very
commonest pewter and plated tea-pots, sugar-bowls, &c.,
inferior prints and woollen goods, and a large collection of
dirty old straw-hats—these represented England and various
other "foreign parts."   I trust all these may speedily be
burnt or packed away, and their places more worthily filled.

One of the most interesting native institutions in Tokio is
the "Dai Gakko," or Imperial university.   The buildings are
large and extend over a wide area.   There are a hundred
and thirty-two resident pupils from twenty years of age
upwards, and the courses of study run from three to four
years according to the special course selected.   There are
five sections, each of which claims the whole study time

of the allotted period. These five sections are science, engineering, law, literature, and medicine. We went over various laboratories and a whole vestibule of small rooms where dissection and the study of disease-germs was being carried on by individual students.

The dormitories for the residents were certainly very rough and rather untidy. Three students sleep in each room, which is fitted up with an iron bedstead and a rough wash-stand for each young man. There was no carpet, and the floor was not very clean. Rich and poor alike study at this college. There are also three hundred and thirty non-residents who attend the lectures. The course is certainly very cheap, and no doubt the instruction is very good, although the arrangements are so rough. Twelve to fifteen yen (1l. 16s. to 2l. 5s.) a month is all that is paid for board, clothing, and instruction. Government must of course subsidize the college very highly, or it could not possibly be self-supporting.

We went into one building here which is set apart for the study of earthquakes, with all the newest instruments for determining the force and course of these disturbances. Some ingenious wire models made by the young Japanese student who showed us over this department gave the convolutions of the disturbance at various seconds during an earthquake. He told me with pride that he was about to forward the results of his observations to Cambridge, in England.

In one of the rooms of the Dai Gakko, we were fortunate enough to meet with a number of Ainos (the natives of the north island of Japan), who had been brought down for some special purposes. Several of these were patriarchal-looking, grey-headed old men of quite different type to any of those found in other parts of Japan, being much larger and more powerful. There were also several women, on a much larger scale than the little "Jap" women, who were partially tattooed with a long straight black line put on for eyebrows and meeting between the eyes.

The women looked sulky and rather morose, but the dear old men were charming. They were sitting upon some high benches in the lecture-room when we entered, but instantly scrambled down, looking so pleased and excited, and salaaming with both hands in a peculiar fashion of their own, which consisted in opening the hands outward towards us with a grand sweep. I noticed that they had very fine and well developed heads. We were lucky to come upon them, for no Ainos had been seen in Tokio for five years previously.

Another wet morning was devoted to going over one of the normal schools, where we saw a number of little Japanese boys and girls drilling and gymnasticising (to coin a word) with native teachers, dressed alas! in European costume. This does not at all suit the Japanese. Would that they could be brought to believe it! The men looked cramped and uncomfortable; the women slouchy and untidy—a great contrast to the effect of their own graceful native dress.

In the pretty garden we noticed as elsewhere the beautiful custom of training wistaria with interlacing poles of bamboo over a considerable space of ground, which is thus roofed over to protect the children from the rays of the sun. When the leaves and flowers are out together, the effect is like fairyland, branches of the blossom dropping down between the interstices of these exquisite green " screens " overhead.

Indoors, we saw several classes going on where the native teachers were giving their lessons in Japanese. One young Japanese girl was teaching her class to sing " at sight " in the European fashion, a decided improvement upon the music we had heard a few days previously in the tea-house. There were four hundred in this school, in addition to two hundred in another building set apart for the smaller children, who are taught upon the kindergarten principle, and were marching round the elliptical circle as sun, moon, and stars ; several little Japanese planets getting very much out of their respective orbits as they wandered on, staring with all their might at the " white devils."

A handsome little boy whom we had noticed playing in the garden with a sword at his side and a cavalier hat, turned out to be a young American, whose mother, or " *mam-ma* " as he called her, was one of the teachers. She came over here eight months ago from Chicago with a two years' engagement. She seemed a very pleasant, intelligent woman, much interested in both her profession and her present pupils. She says that most of the normal pupils are educated by Government free of expense, on the understanding that they should become teachers, the boys binding themselves to teach for ten years, and the girls for five years, after their education is completed. The shorter term for women is doubtless designed that they may not be too old to marry when released from their agreement. Some have eluded the responsibility by leaving just before their own education is completed, but this is a rare occurrence, and is naturally considered a dishonourable one.

I paid a visit later to a lady whose advent in Japan from England had been the subject of general discussion for some weeks before our visit to Tokio. She had come with a staff of six lady teachers, at the instigation of the Japanese Government, to start a high class school for the education of the daughters of the Japanese nobility. The school is to be under the management of a committee of Japanese gentlemen, and the lady principal begged that I would not enter into any further details, as she had promised to send home no reports of the work. It was easy to make the promise, for at the time of our visit there was absolutely nothing to see except the quaint picturesque old home, formerly the residence of a 'daimio," where the experiment was to be made.

It would be impossible to leave Tokio without paying a visit to Sengakuji (the Hill Spring Temple), made famous as the burial-place of the "forty-seven Ronins." The temple is prettily situated about a mile from the town, and on a fine day the drive there would have been beautiful. As it was, in pouring rain, we had only the beauty of association. The romantic story has been so well told by Mr. Mitford in his *Tales of Old Japan*, that it seems needless to give even a slight sketch of it here. Some, however, may not have read it, whilst others may be glad to have their memories refreshed.

The lord of these forty-seven heroes had failed in some slight point of etiquette on a state occasion at the court of one of the Shoguns. He was young and inexperienced, and the matter would have been passed over without comment, but another courtier who was jealous of him had taunted and insulted the hot-headed youth. The latter in a fit of righteous indignation drew his sword and wounded his enemy. For this offence he was condemned to commit *hara-kiri*. This mode of death (which allowed the criminal to disembowel himself) was only accorded as a great privilege and honour where there was nothing absolutely dishonourable in the nature of the crime committed.

The deceased was buried at Sengakuji. Fifty-three of his vassals, headed by Kuranoski (his secretary), agreed amongst themselves to avenge his death by killing the man who had insulted him and so caused his untimely end. In order to avoid suspicion and throw the enemy off guard, they dispersed themselves over the country, ever faithful to the object in view. A year was allowed to pass before Kuranoski met his comrades in Yedo (Tokio). The number was reduced by this time to forty-six, the rest having died. One night they attacked the house of their enemy, and after killing many of his retainers, cut off his head and carried it in triumph to

Sengakuji where they washed it in the well which is still to
be seen outside the cemetery, and then placed it on the tomb
of their beloved lord and master.

After this tragedy, they gave themselves up to Government, and in consideration of the nature of their offence, they
also were allowed to die the death of honour by committing
hara-kiri. They cheerfully obeyed the order, dying before
the grave of their lord.

We counted forty-seven upright stones which stand round
a small square not much bigger than a dining-room table.
The forty-seventh belongs to a Satsuma man, who had insulted
and spat upon Kuranoski, thinking that the latter had given
up his intention of avenging his master. Kuranoski pre-
tended to be lying drunk and helpless in the streets, which
accounted for the misunderstanding, he having done so only
to further his own schemes by secrecy. The man who had
done the secretary such injustice endeavoured to make
atonement and to show his admiration for Kuranoski by
committing *hara-kiri* before his tomb.

It is a touching story, and shows us that men of all
nations and in all times have been found willing "to die
for a sentiment." No one would wish to dim the glory of
our Christian martyrs, but it is as well to remember that
the "poor degraded heathen" upon whom some of us look
with pity not unmixed by contempt, have sometimes died
deaths casting quite as radiant a glory around them in
proportion to the amount of light they have received.

CHAPTER VI.

JAPAN (*continued*).

THE rainy season in Japan was now (June) in full force, and
much calculation and patience were necessary to utilize the
few fine days in the best possible manner. Of course the
rain is much needed, as this is the "rice-sowing" season, one
harvest being gathered in whilst the other is sown. From
the tourist's point of view, however, the rain is a nuisance,
and it is difficult to decide upon which is the best time to
visit Japan. A late winter makes travelling difficult until

April has set in. Sometimes early rains will fall even in this month. The legitimate rainy season begins in May and continues till early July, and then the heat becomes too great for comfort in travelling. I think, on the whole, the autumn must be the best season for a trip to Japan. A traveller at that season of the year loses the spring flowers but sees the chrysanthemums in full glory; the rains and heat are things of the past, and the roads are dry and hard, with a brilliant sun overhead and a fresh, crisp feeling in the air.

Go when you will, each month is famous for some special flower. If you miss one, it is only to find others in greater beauty, in this favoured land.

We took advantage of a tolerably fine day to start from Yokohama for a two days' expedition to Kamakura and home by Enoshima. Most people go there and back in the day and partly by train, thus missing the most beautiful part of the expedition. We engaged 'rickshas for the whole trip, but had great difficulty in persuading our coolies to go by one road and return by another.

They wished naturally to take us by the longer but less hilly road which we traversed next day on our return journey. Great firmness gained the day. Otherwise we should have gone over the same road twice, missing all the finest scenery.

The road was certainly bad, but this was chiefly owing to the heavy rains which had just fallen. Of course, having gained our point, we felt bound in honour to walk up all the hills and relieve the poor coolies as much as possible.

We started across the fields, a terribly heavy road, rising by slight degrees until we reached Seki, where a pause was made, and whence we walked a good distance to the beautiful pass amongst the hills, overlooking Kanazawa and the Plains of Heaven. A glorious panorama of fertile plains, intersecting streams, blue mountains on the horizon line, and deep blue sea lay below us. Every shade of green in the trees adding variety and colour to the enchanting view. Further on still, is a spot called Nokendo, where upon an eminence is built a small tea-house, close to a remarkable looking old pine-tree. The story goes that the famous Japanese artist Kanaoka tried to paint the view from here, but threw away his brush in despair of ever being able to do justice to it. Drinking in the sugarless, milkless, Japanese tea and the beauty around us at the same time, we felt that any other great artist might have a similar experience!

Kanazawa is a lovely and picturesque spot which lay in the valley beneath us, on a stretch of land between the mountains.

It is famous for the peonies which grow here on trees of several feet in height. We saw the trees, but the flowers, alas! were over. These peonies measure from eight to fifteen inches in diameter.

To make up for our disappointment we saw hundreds of lovely white tiger lilies, growing quite wild all over the fields and hills in this vicinity. All flowers; chrysanthemums, camellias, roses, peonies, and lilies, grow in great profusion here at the proper seasons of the year.

After passing Kanazawa, we reached Kamakura (which also lies in a valley inclosed by hills) about five o'clock in the afternoon.

Kamakura was formerly the eastern and political capital of Japan. It is now a mere straggling village with little trace of its ancient glory. One splendid temple, however, remains as a relic of the past—the Temple of Hachiman, which is built on a commanding position, showing its red roofs amongst the dark green trees surrounding it.

The Shogun Yoritomo made this spot the military capital in A.D. 1185, and the ground is full of traditions concerning him and the Minamoto family from which he sprang.

The temple rests on a plateau, reached by climbing fifty-eight steps. It is full of relics of this Shogun. Several beautifully carved and ornamented swords are kept here which belonged to him—also his helmet, covered with gold dragons, and his hunting suit of many-coloured silks, now "tattered and torn."

These were shown to us by the priests, with great pride. There is a grand specimen here of a tree, which had puzzled us for some time in other places. It has a curious leaf, like a gigantic maiden-hair fern. The tree is a great height and very full in foliage, and this particular specimen is said to be a thousand years old, but looked far too fresh and green and strong for such antiquity.

It is called the *Salisburia Adiantifolia*, and must belong to the maiden-hair family.

A grandson of Yoritomo is said to have stood beneath this very tree, disguised as a girl (1218 A.D.), to kill his uncle Sanetomo, a Minister of State, who had connived at the death of his own brother (the boy's father), Kugio, in order to gain this official post.

Some inclosed stones near the entrance to the temple are said to be sacred, and to have wonderful properties. Like the man in Mark Twain's *Jumping Frog*, I did "not see any points about them more than any other stones," but barren women come here to pray for offspring, and also members of both sexes to ask for suitable partners for life.

On the other side of the town of Kamakura is the grand bronze image of Buddha—the Dai Butsu. This colossal seated figure is placed in the open air, with a background of trees and foliage, and is the most wonderful and glorious work of art in all Japan. Nothing but the Sphynx and the colossal Osiri of Aboo Simbel in Egypt ever made such an impression upon me.

In size, it is second only to the gigantic Nara image of Buddha, but the latter is inclosed in a temple, and does not "begin to compare" with this one in beauty of conception.

This seated figure is fifty feet in height; the face is eight feet long, the ear six feet six inches, the nostrils three feet wide, the mouth three feet eight inches wide.

These calculations give some idea of the size, but are powerless to convey any impression of the marvellous beauty of the face itself.

It is truly the Human—*informed* and uplifted by the Divine—patient, far-seeing, satisfied. Looking at it, you feel you could sit there day by day and never tire, nor come away otherwise than soothed and helped by the atmosphere of sublime repose. It seemed to me that I had lost something out of my life when we drove past next morning, catching one last glimpse of this marvel on our way to Enoshima, an island or peninsula according to the state of the tide.

Our route thither lay first by the village of Sakanoshta, where we struck the beach and a very beautiful but tempestuous-looking sea. Tradition says that in the year 1333 A.D., Nitta Yoshida, the brave vassal of the Mikado Godaigo, was sent against the powerful forces of Hojo, lord of Kamakura.

At this spot he received a check by perceiving a fleet of war galleys which blocked his sea passage, whilst an overpowering army prevented his progress by land. Nitta, in despair, sacrificed to the *Kami* (gods), and threw into the

waves, as an offering, a magnificent sword given to him by
the Emperor. That evening the tide ebbed, and by early
morning the galleys were far out at sea, too far to harm
Nitta and his followers, who, thus encouraged, were easily
led to victory on land. Kamakura was taken, and Hojo's
power was at an end.

Walking along this sea-shore whilst our 'rickshas were
dragged heavily along by the coolies, we had the most
glorious views of Fuji-yama, rising up in splendour alone
from the plain. The graceful sweeping lines of the sacred
mountain can only be seen to advantage from this neighbourhood, but we were peculiarly fortunate in our day.

A friend whom we met later at Enoshima, told us that he
had been four times on the road within a few weeks, but
had never seen the view so well before.

Enoshima stands far out in the sea, being connected with
Katase, a dirty little town on the mainland, by a narrow strip
of ground which is generally under water. A boat took us
across, and we landed on the "island" pick-a-back in most
ungraceful fashion. One steep little street forms the whole
town of Enoshima, and the shops display some very ingenious pictures made with shells, representing birds, trees,
houses, &c.

The real curiosity of Enoshima, however, is the *Hosu-gai*,
a rare and very interesting sponge, which grows with its glassy
cable (exactly like spun glass) downwards, and is only found
in very deep waters at some distance from the coast.

Getting back into the boat was far worse than the landing had been. I had to jump on to the back of my poor little Jap as if I were going to play " leap-frog," and then we were literally *rolled over the side* of the boat into position.

As the day remained fine, we drove the whole way back to Yokohama by the Tokaido road, instead of taking the railway as we might have done at a certain point on our return.

Another of our few fine days, we went by steamer to Yokoska, on the opposite side of the harbour from Yokohama, and due south of it. This place is reached in about two hours by water. The sail was very charming, but the steamers as usual very uncomfortable. The one idea of the Japanese is to push all the women into a stuffy cabin whence no view can possibly be obtained. The alternative is to sit upon your heels, amongst the Japs themselves, on an upper deck, to which you must scramble over boxes and rice barrels (*koku*) as best you may.

We chose the latter course invariably ; but the absence of any "back-rest" is very painful to European female nature.

The interest of Yokoska is supposed to lie in the fact that Will Adams, a celebrated English pilot, and his Japanese wife are buried here. It is well worth while to make the very steep ascent of forty minutes, up one of the highest hills, to the mounds where these stone graves are situated. I am afraid I took more interest in the exquisite beauty of the view thus obtained than in

the association with Will Adams, never having heard of
that individual before going to Japan. It seems that he
was an English pilot, who set out, about the year 1607, to
join a fleet of ships in Holland, for trading purposes with
Japan. The enterprise was most disastrous. Boisterous
weather came on. The crews suffered terribly; and only
one of the fleet, with Adams on board, reached her destination. Their troubles did not end here, for the survivors
were treated at first with great cruelty by the natives.

Adams, however, thanks to his knowledge of ship-
building and mathematics, became a great favourite with
the Shogun of those days, who conferred upon him some
land and an annual revenue of rice. In spite of these
advantages, he was naturally anxious to return to his
wife and children in England, but the Japanese authorities
would not hear of this. Being a philosopher, apparently,
he made the best of things, took a Japanese wife, by
whom he had two children, and eventually chose this most
exquisite spot for his grave. The tombs and stone lanterns
were put up by his neighbours, and his memory is still
held in greatest reverence by the natives, many of whom
claim to be descended from him.

The little town of Yokoska is dusty and dirty, and only
famous for its grand naval arsenal buildings, where we saw
some fine ships in course of construction. Many visitors
unfortunately never get beyond the town. The steep
climb daunts some. They are willing to take "Will

Adams" on trust, and do not realize what they miss in the superb view from his tombstone.

An interesting expedition to me personally, lies within easy reach of Yokohama, taking the train to Kanagawa (the first station on the line to Tokio), and thence by the sea-coast for a mile and a half, to a lonely mound by the roadside, where a plain slab of stone, with Japanese inscription, marks the resting-place of Mr. Richardson. My special interest lies in the fact of knowing his niece, but the sad tragedy of his death, in 1862, is a matter of Japanese history.

All will remember how this hot-headed young Englishman defied a Japanese prince, when requested to make room for him, and dismount when he passed, and how the former was instantly cut down by the infuriated Japanese retainers, when he refused obedience to the order in terms of unmeasured contempt. He was one of a riding party, who had set out that morning against the advice of friends, who knew that this Japanese noble was likely to come into the city that day, and that foreigners unwilling to show him the customary signs of respect would be safer out of the way.

The poor young fellow, with all an Englishman's insular obstinacy and contempt for any authority outside his native country, declined to recognize any "miserable Japanese" idea of rank or superiority. Many blame his conduct as overbearing and indiscreet. No doubt it was both, but he paid a heavy price for acting as many other young Englishmen would have done in his place, thinking the honour of their country was at stake.

"Black-eyed Susan"—the faithful young Japanese girl who hid the wounded man, and nursed him till he died—still lives in a tea-house close by the scene of his death. She is a middle-aged woman now, forty-six years old, and it was difficult to realize in her the heroine of this romantic episode. The English Government took up the matter very sternly, and the Japanese were forced to pay the heavy sum of £125,000 as compensation for the death of a British subject.

A very pleasant excursion from Yokohama is to Miyanoshta, which a friend of mine describes as "the Simla" of Japan. It is an inland watering-place within easy reach of the capital, and most romantically situated amongst the mountains. We spent a week here, and enjoyed ourselves very much in spite of some rainy days.

The Fujiya hotel, where we came to anchor, is charmingly placed on the very edge of the mountain, and surrounded by beautiful gardens full of azaleas at the time of our visit.

There are capital sulphur baths to be had in the hotel, which are extremely refreshing and soothing, and most efficacious in skin diseases.

The Japanese suffer terribly from this curse, and making the steep ascent to Miyanoshta we passed and met many Japanese being carried in *kagos* to this place of healing.

Of course they stay as a rule in native tea-houses, but

there are two very good hotels for Europeans, and many, both Japanese and Europeans, spend weeks during the summer months in this beautiful mountain retreat.

There are some fine walks to be taken in the neighbourhood, and the wild flowers delighted my eyes on every side. Wild spiræa—a species of the "dogwood" tree so common in California—wild white roses in clusters, deutzia, purple columbine, wild honeysuckle, and a dwarf rhododendron somewhat resembling the Alpenrosen of Switzerland,—these are only a few of the many beauties we found in our daily walks. One of the chief attractions of Miyanoshta is the expedition to be made on a fine day from here to the Otomi Pass, whence a glorious view of Fuji-yama is obtained.

We made many attempts to get there, but on each occasion the clouds descended at the most critical moment, and to go there on a wet day is absolutely useless.

So we consoled ourselves by a rather disappointing excursion to the Hakone Lake—disappointing because, being a sulphurous volcanic district, the hills were very bare of vegetation. We were fully repaid, however, on the other side of the lake, where we ascended the mountains over-hanging a sulphurous valley. We had to scramble down the latter on our feet, passing several boiling sulphur-springs, and admiring the rose and crimson shades of the hills, covered in patches by green trees.

It was a lurid, weird, and yet most picturesque scene. The continuous rains drove us back to Yokohama at last, where we cultivated a little European society, and saw something of the modern social life of the place by attending one or two afternoon dances. One of these was given on board the American flag-ship the *Brooklyn*, to commemorate the glorious "Fourth of July." A dance on board ship is always made pretty by flowers and flags, but is seldom successful for non-dancers, who seem to be even more in the way here than on dry land.

We finished up the afternoon by driving with some friends to see a native garden where hundreds of the little dwarf trees for which Japan is so famous are to be found.

Many of these trees, firs, yews, &c., are from sixty to seventy years old, perfectly developed, but only a foot high, and proportionately small in circumference. They are artificially trained by clipping, cutting, and being kept in dark cellars, with just light enough for life, but not for *development*. What a sad type of many human lives! I could not bear to look at them. They reminded me so much of poor little dwarfs reared on gin! The gentleman with whom we had visited this garden insisted upon taking us to a friend's house to tea. The host and hostess were both absent, but he assured us this made no difference, so we calmly walked in by his invitation, and presently tea was brought to us on the veranda.

By and by, some gentlemen who had been presented to me on board the *Brooklyn* strayed in, found us there, and remained also for tea.

Going away, we met the host and his wife returning from their drive, but they passed us too quickly for more than a hasty bow to our friend. It seemed to me so delightfully un-English! Imagine two sets of people in an English town straying into another person's house, finding no one at home, and all of them quietly remaining for tea and rest on their friend's veranda!

I should recommend all travellers who can do so, to plan their Japanese tour as we did, from west to east, entering the country at the Kioto end, and finishing up with the wonders of Nikko. Otherwise everything will be apt to appear "flat, stale, and unprofitable." After the glorious Nikko temples, and the beauty of the vicinity, the real charms of Kioto will not be appreciated as they deserve.

Nikko, literally and metaphorically, "takes the colour out" of everything else in Japan, and should therefore be kept as a *bonne bouche* at the end of the feast—or to change this very mixed metaphor, good amateur singing may give immense pleasure, but we shall scarcely be prepared to do full justice to it as a sequel to one of Patti's divine airs.

Knowing all this we had put off Nikko to the last, intending to take it quietly and enjoy ourselves fully, instead of making the hasty rush through that seems to satisfy the ordinary tourist.

We soon found, alas! one or two good reasons for such

a speedy return; for the accommodation in this exquisite spot is very bad.

But I will describe this our last expedition at some length. Nikko was to form part of an eighteen days' trip into the interior of Japan, and having engaged a guide from Yokohama, we spent one night again at Tokio in order to make final arrangements, and lay in a stock of potted meats and soups sufficient to last us for the time required.

The most trying point in Japanese travel is the terrible want of sleep which an ordinary traveller must face, more especially in the summer season. Out of the eighteen days spent on this particular expedition, for example, I never had more than three or at most four hours' sleep on any night, and for nights together one lay awake for hours; first dozing off towards daylight, in time to make the early rise and early start, a real affliction.

Some few happy people are impervious to all noises and every other drawback, but I am sure that most travellers will bear out my statement to some degree; although I trust few will have had an identical experience, for I am peculiarly unfortunate in being a very nervous sleeper at all times.

But I believe the Seven Sleepers themselves would have woke up sometimes in Japan !

The disturbances are so many and so great.

Frogs croaking, fleas jumping, mosquitoes biting; add to these the noises of men and women, especially when they pull the heavy outside wooden shutters to and fro, late at night and by cockcrow in the morning, just when, fairly exhausted by a long night's campaign with the fleas, you may be just dropping for the first time into an uneasy slumber.

Leaving Tokio at midday, we reached Utsonimiya in three hours, and there engaged our 'rickshas for the four hours drive to Nikko. The rail went as usual through an uninteresting part of the country. The day was dull and foggy, but began without actual rain.

The drive to Nikko lies through avenues upon avenues of fir, ilex, and cryptomeria; the latter, a splendid species of pine which grows just here in great profusion and to an immense height, some of the trees measuring from 150 to 200 feet. They grow so straight that the wood is very much used in making the masts of ships.

We admired the avenues immensely at first, but the absolute monotony of scene became wearisome.

Then the rain began ; drizzling at first but becoming more severe every few minutes.

We reached Nikko at length, tired, hungry, and wet, about 8 P.M., when it was too dark to see anything of the town. Our guide insisted upon taking us to see the "Suzuki" tea-house, just before crossing the two bridges of Nikko. A mile further on, over the bridge and up the hill, is "Kanaya's" tea-house, which is small but much pleasanter in every way, being cleaner and far more beautifully situated.

We went in to see it next day, and should have insisted

upon moving up there, but unfortunately the rooms were all engaged by some Russian celebrities who were coming to spend some weeks in the neighbourhood.

As this house is so superior but limited in accommodation, it would be well for other travellers to engage rooms beforehand.

The guides are not likely to look with favour on such a proceeding, as Kanaya, having a good reputation, and large *clientèle*, probably gives them no commission upon the travellers brought to his house. Suzuki must evidently do so, for no one in his senses could otherwise compare the two tea-houses, as our own guide did, to the disadvantage of the smaller one. The "red lacquer bridge" of Nikko is close to Suzuki's, and has the usual legend attached to it.

A "holy man," Shodo Shonin, came here and found the rocks so steep, and the whirlpools between them so rapid and dangerous, that a crossing seemed quite impossible.

He prayed, however, to Buddha and the gods, and immediately saw faint outlines of the god Shinsa Daio holding two red and green snakes which he cast into the abyss. In an instant a long bridge floated across like a rainbow amongst the hills, and the holy man passed over it in safety.

The present bridge was built in 1635, and is eighty-four feet long by eighteen feet wide. It is closed at both ends by locks.

In olden times only the Shoguns were allowed to pass over

this sacred bridge. The privilege is now reserved for the Mikado.

In spite of the most pronounced "anti-boring" principles, I find it impossible to write of gorgeous Nikko without saying something more of the temples which are here seen to the greatest advantage. One of the finest of these is the "To Sho Gu," approached by a grand avenue of cryptomeria trees.

Words fail to describe the garden of this temple. It is "depraved Shinto" in style; that is to say, Shinto which has lost its simplicity and taken on Buddhist decoration, but escaping the gaudiness which marks so many of the true Buddhist temples.

The carvings in wood of dragons, birds, storks, pheasants, &c., are coloured in beautiful shades of green, pink, white, crimson, and cream.

The best of these were done by the celebrated left-handed artist, Hidari Jingoro.

Many buildings are grouped together on this temple ground. First and foremost, on a raised platform, is the wonderful Yomei-Mon, or Dream Gate, a marvel of gilding and carving; beautiful indeed as a dream. This gate has a double row of gilded dragons all round it, each dragon opening its mouth in a different way from all the others.

We came back again and again to this exquisite Dream Gate, and never wearied of discovering fresh wonders of colour and carving in its sublime grandeur.

The Buddhist scriptures are kept in a splendid revolving lacquer shrine, each compartment of which opens, revealing numerous little drawers full of holy manuscript.

Two handsome "drum towers" contain the drums beaten to call worshippers to the temple. Here also are to be seen a fine bronze candelabra, given by the King of Riukiu, and an equally handsome bronze bell, the gift of the King of Corea, and nicknamed the "Moth-eaten Bell" on account of a hole in the bronze.

Every bit of stone wall around these buildings is covered with red, green, or blue painting over the stone trellis-work, the interstices being filled in with wonderful carvings in painted wood of fabulous dragons, combined with birds, beasts, and fishes.

The most gorgeous building of all is the central one, which is one mass of grand colouring, lacquer, and bronze.

This building has lovely bamboo curtains raised by thick cream-coloured cords, and is so crowded with exquisite bronze and lacquer ornaments, &c., that it is hopeless to give any idea of its marvels.

I noticed specially some small lacquer pillars, as hard as bronze, and made *entirely* of lacquer, one coating placed upon the other. This is the most expensive work in Japan, each of these pillars having cost two millions of dollars !

The wood-work of all these buildings is lacquered over with a beautiful crimson shade that forms an exquisite contrast to the background of the trees.

The temple of "To Sho Gu" is specially famous as the shrine of Iyeyasu, the celebrated Shogun, who gave peace to his country for two hundred and seventy years by winning a decisive battle. His tomb lies two hundred feet above the temple. It is as usual of plain bronze in cupola form, and with handsome bronze gates in front.

The other grand Nikko temple is dedicated to Iyemitsu, and likewise consecrated to the Shinto form of worship. It is crowded with exquisite wood carvings, lacquer, and gilding, but not being quite so gorgeous as "To Sho Gu," I have chosen the latter to describe at greater length.

There is a curious monument to Iyemitsu, a high bronze pillar, with tiny bronze bells hanging round it, very graceful, and quite different from most of the Shogun monuments.

Another temple in these grounds is dedicated to the goddess and patroness of children (Kishibojin), who is said to have had a thousand children herself, so should certainly know something about the care of them. Another red-lacquer building contains the bones of Yoritomo, but as these are kept carefully in a tiny gold shrine under an image of Buddha, we were forced to take them on trust.

The real charm of the Japanese temples begins when the sight-seeing is over, and you are free to feast your eyes on the graceful outlines of these gilded and dark-brown or dark-crimson tiled roofs, blending with the various shades of moss-grown stone steps, and the beautiful cryptomeria, pines, and other fir-trees which surround them.

On the second day of our visit to Nikko, we had our first experience of the famous *kago*, which is used for mountain excursions, where neither the jinricksha nor a bamboo-chair are possible means of conveyance. The *kago* looks exactly like a round wicker tea-tray, slung by bamboo supports on to a stout bamboo pole, which is borne by a coolie at each end. A thin plaited bamboo roof protects the wretched inmate from the outside sun. The tiny little Japanese men and women fit comfortably enough into these instruments of torture, sitting cross-legged in Turkish fashion.

But the poor European has a bad time in one of them! You must scramble in sideways like a crab, and feel very much like a sick snail when you get there! The pole comes down so low that it is impossible to wear a hat on your head, and the traveller is most uncomfortably close to the ground.

We went about six miles out to a beautiful waterfall, as our "preliminary canter" in *kagos*, for it was necessary to grow accustomed to this mode of conveyance before starting on our combined *kago* and *'ricksha* expedition to Chiusengi Lake, and on to Ikao.

The very moderate demands of the Japanese coolies increase in inverse ratio to the amount of civilization. In the large towns, the prices are low, but once off the beaten track, monopoly as usual runs up the tariff, and we were obliged to be very firm, both with our guide and the coolies, before the bargain could be struck with any sort of self-respect on our side.

It ended in our leaving Nikko one morning with three *kagos*, one for my friend, one for myself, and a third for our little guide. Three men were required for each of our two *kagos*, but our little Jap was so small and light that two men could easily carry him, so the third coolie was utilized to bear our provisions, sheets, towels, food, and pots and pans, and the small baggage absolutely necessary for two nights.

The rest of our very modest belongings were to be sent on next day from Nikko in the 'rickshas which would reach us by another route at the further end of the Copper Mine Pass.

Fuji (our guide) looked like a young boy, but said he was thirty-two years old, and had not only a wife but a little son of nine years old.

He had an odd, abrupt manner, not intentionally rude, but very unlike the "gentle Jap" with whom we had hitherto made acquaintance. It amused us to notice the extraordinary *influence of clothes.* When in his guide dress (true European) he was bluff, abrupt, and rather apt to be sulky.

In the evenings, when the day's work was over and he got into his Japanese *kimona*, a wondrous change came over him. Not only did he look much better, but he became at once more amiable and gentle. We thought of asking him always to put on the *kimona* when places and arrangements had to be made and discussed!

Fuji, however, had some very excellent qualities, and was perhaps none the worse for being a rough diamond. He was extremely careful that we should not over-walk ourselves, saying calmly, when he thought we had had enough exercise, "Now, missus, you come and lie down," which meant another scramble into the *kago*.

The road to Chiusengi is over a mountain pass, a number of rough steps cut into the earth leading up to the top. Fuji declared there were a thousand of these to be climbed, and on my saying mildly, "Oh! Fuji, there *cannot* be a thousand," he answered laconically, "*Can*". I am afraid I laughed instead of scolding him, but the tone was so inimitable, and more like that of a naughty rude child than the father of a family!

We had some grand mountain views from the various spots where we rested in making the ascent. It was very severe work for the *kago* men, but we eased them as much as possible by walking up all the steepest places.

About every two minutes (fifty steps) there is a halt to change shoulders or men; for the third man walks behind and pushes when the other two are carrying the *kago* pole. These various changes are made most amicably, the "off man" being always ready for his turn of "active service."

Going up the steep places, the men keep up a monotonous chant on two notes which sounds like "*Cusho-Cusha, Cusho-Cusha*," the accent being on the first syllable. This seems

P

in some mysterious way to help them. Perhaps on the same principle as the song of the "little bastik" in *Helen's Babies,* which Toddie declared made him feel "all good and nicey inside."

On reaching the magnificent head of the pass, we scrambled down some wooden steps to see a beautiful waterfall, consisting of seven small falls ranged round a precipitous amphitheatre of rocks about 700 feet high.

These rocks are serrated at the edges in the most curious way, exactly as if some giant had taken a huge pair of scissors and *snipped* them into V shapes. The colouring is of every varied tint of rose-colour and grey.

A fringe of the *snipped* rock hangs over the chasm with very strange effect.

Thousands of tiny birds circle round this beautiful amphitheatre, getting a bath now and again in the waters that flow down the rocky sides in seven or eight distinct streams.

We reached Chiusengi, and had our first view of the lovely lake about four o'clock in the afternoon.

Mountains clothed in verdure rose up on all sides. The whole length of the sheet of water is about six and a half miles, but the small villages and tea-houses are quite at the upper end of the lake, and it narrows so much just below these that we could only see from the windows of our tea-house the circular portion nearest to us.

We had brought our own sheets and made our own beds,

for the natives do not understand the European way of putting on sheets.

A wide veranda stretching in front of our rooms "gave" on to the lake, and here we dined, watching the beautiful sunset effects over the mountains and the calm blue water at our feet.

Salmon trout from the lake, a very skinny chicken which we had seen "drawn" and then washed in the lake after our arrival (killed also, I should imagine, from its toughness), and some horrible coffee made from the paste which Fuji insisted upon bringing with him, formed our modest meal.

Fleas abounded as usual, but the mosquitoes mercifully were conspicuous by their absence.

Next day we made an expedition to the neighbouring lake of Yumoto, much frequented by the natives for its sulphur baths.

Passing along a fine wide plain, with glorious mountain views, we ascended by degrees to the Dragon Waterfall, so called from the shape of the rocks over which the water falls.

Carpets of the most gorgeous azaleas in deep crimsons, white, and pink, and with monster blossoms, surrounded us; for in these high regions the flower was just then in fullest bloom.

Further on, we came upon another grand waterfall, coming sheer down over an almost perpendicular slab of granite, 600 feet in height.

Azaleas, purple and lemon columbine, tree hydrangeas, and feathery white deutzia lined our road.

It was well to have so much beauty to make us forget the jolting misery of the *kagos*.

A very steep ascent from the last fall brought us shortly to the little village of Yumoto, situated at the head of a lake of that name, which is about two and a half miles long.

Fuji was most anxious that we should have a sulphur bath, but threatening weather had delayed our start, and we had no time for more than a stroll through the village to the source of the sulphur spring.

Men, women, and children, were sitting happily together in public baths along the road; these baths being square inclosures fed by bamboo aqueducts from the sulphur spring. No conventional ideas of propriety seem to arise to spoil the happiness and comfort of these little family parties. It is Eden before the Fall and the Fig-leaves.

On the return to Chiusengi, we left our *kagos* with great delight after two hours, and came back to Chiusengi in a boat across the lovely lake. Lake Chiusengi is 3,700 feet above the sea-level, and eight miles long. High mountains inclose it on every side, the village nestling at the foot of Nantaisan, one of the holy mountains of Japan, 9,000 feet high, and which "divides honours" with Fuji-yama.

Another night of croaking frogs and biting fleas, brought us to the morning, when we were to start for the Copper Mine Pass.

A boat took us and our *kagos* across the Chiusengi Lake, and thence up and over the magnificent scenery of the Copper Mine Pass, into the very heart of the glorious mountains. We walked down the other side of the Pass by the Copper Mine Mountain, which is being extensively worked. Smelting furnaces are built on the sides of the mountain, and a long series of aqueducts convey the water needed for "washing" the metal. The copper is sent off direct to Osaka to be converted into coin at the Osaka mint.

Two more hours in the *kagos* brought us to a shed where we found the 'rickshas which had been sent on for us the previous day from Nikko.

We got into them with great delight, but, alas! it was "out of the frying-pan into the fire." The road was terribly rough, and the jolting of the 'ricks in proportion to it.

The scenery of the Aseo Pass was so magnificent, however, that we were in a constant state of excitement and delight, in spite of our poor suffering bodies.

We had found the 'ricks at 11 A.M., but did not reach Omama (our sleeping-place) till 8 P.M., by which time it was quite dark for our drive through the endless Japanese village to our quarters for the night.

A dirty little tea-house devoured by fleas—that is all I remember of Omama when I arose after a sleepless night with a lively remembrance of the fatigues of the preceding day.

Some three or four hours over comparatively tame scenery

and a series of rice-fields brought us to Mayebashi, where we were once more within reach of civilization. All through this district the silk business is carried on very extensively.

Thousands of cocoons are drying before the houses of the native villages, and the fine white silk is being reeled off by wooden machines, which fly round in the hands of pretty young Jap girls or withered old Jap women.

The mulberry-trees which abound here are smaller than ours, and the leaves are more pointed.

The fruit also is dwarfed, owing to the constant stripping of the leaves in the interest of the silk looms.

After lunch and a rest at Mayebashi, we had still six hours more in our 'ricks before reaching Ikao, where we had agreed to spend two or three days. The heat was intense, and the last three or four miles were on a constant ascent; mercifully through shady woods, but a very trying road, being all what is technically called " collar work."

Several coolies had fallen off during the day, sick from the great heat and from drinking too much cold water. No wonder, poor creatures! Their first idea on entering a village is to bury their heads in a tub of water, drinking down all they can and soaking their handkerchiefs in the rest. Later on these same handkerchiefs are wrung out over and over again after being passed over their hot bodies and faces.

It is a hard life, and the coolie class is said to be very improvident. They lay nothing by for old age, which comes very quickly on them, for at thirty or forty a coolie is no longer able to run at the pace required. Heart disease is very prevalent amongst them, as might easily be imagined.

The crown of beautiful mountains surrounding the little village of Ikao looked very lovely in the setting sun, with glorious billows of crimson and gold clouds standing far out from the sky, and a tiny young moon peeping forth for the first time as we came to the end of our long day's journey.

Oh! the luxury of a room to one's self and a wash-stand, no matter how primitive, *inside* of it. Hitherto my friend and I had been forced to adjourn to the open veranda and do our washing there, pitching the water down from the tin basin for the next one to fill again, and in view of an admiring crowd of spectators, chiefly men. At Ikao, although the rooms are divided by screens in tea-house fashion, European customs obtain sufficiently for a wash-stand to be placed inside the room.

Ikao boasts of an iron spring and iron baths, which are hot and extremely pleasant.

Bands of cotton steeped in the iron water and coloured like iron mould are sold in the little village, and much esteemed for their tonic effect.

It is a dirty little village, built on the side of a hill, but commanding magnificent views of the mountains opposite.

Ikao possesses two hotels, and we chose the higher of these on account of the view.

Our first day there was spent in sorely needed rest, lounging on cane chairs in our veranda, watching the magnificent mountains and—mending our clothes!

On the second day, my friend elected to remain quiet again, so I started off alone, with guide and coolies, for Haruna, and was rewarded by seeing some of the most beautiful scenery in Japan.

The expedition embraces a lake, some glorious mountain views, and a romantic little temple amongst the rocks at the end of it. The distance is only eight miles, but the ground is very steep, and we took three hours to get there, including rests at the various tea-houses *en route.*

A naval officer from the American flag- ship *Brooklyn* was in a sedan chair just in front of me on his way to join a friend at the first tea-house, whence they were to ascend one of the highest mountains in the district. He came forward very pleasantly with a " Good morning, madam. I presume you are about to proceed to Haruna ? " and we chatted very comfortably for ten minutes whilst my coolies rested. How thoroughly un-English! and yet how sensible to break the monotony of the long day for both of us!

If an Englishman had attempted to do it, he would have failed through *mauvaise honte,* or the fear that the lady might resent it as an impertinence. Certainly " they manage these things better in America."

After an hour's ascent, I reached the tea-house, whence the grandest view is obtained, and hence a descent of three-

quarters of an hour brought us to the quaint little Haruna
Temple, built amongst some very curious rocks.

Some of these are shaped like bridges, others like the
saddle and bridle of a horse, &c. One, called the Candle Rock,
rises to a height of one hundred and fifty feet, and is almost
perpendicular. Fuji assured me that twice a year the priest
climbs up here (although there is no footing visible) to take
up some of the "holy paper" used in Shinto worship, leaving
it about two-thirds up the rock, where there is a little ledge
in the stone. No one else could possibly do it, but the "holy
man" has done it for years and never hurt himself.

My little guide declared that he had witnessed the performance several times. Looking at the rock and hearing the
"miracle," I could only say as the Duke of Wellington is
reported to have done, "Well, as you tell me it is so, of course
I believe it; but I can assure you that had I seen it myself I
should not have believed it!"

I returned to Ikao quite charmed with the Haruna expedition, which turned out to be the very last really *delightful* day
that I spent in Japan.

Next morning we left Ikao, and returning pretty much on
our former track, reached the Itsuka Station in about three
hours, where my friend and I were to separate for a week.

She had had enough of the roughness and discomfort of
Japanese travel, and determined to go back to Yokohama
instead of completing the tour, which had been arranged
to take in Lake Suwa on the Nakasendo road.

Innumerable travellers had spoken of the extreme

beauty of this road, warning us against the chance of missing it, and all had insisted upon the fact that the chief beauty lay to the *east* of the lake.

Having determined to penetrate so far at least, I made up my mind to carry out the programme and go on alone with the guide and the coolies.

The expedition proved a lamentable disappointment, and on this occasion Fortune certainly did not favour the brave. The little I shall write of my experiences in this portion of the "heart of Japan" is intended rather as a warning than as an example to go and do likewise. The Nakasendo road is doubtless beautiful in some parts, but those parts must lie on the Kioto side and between that city and Lake Suwa, and not between Tokio and the lake as we had been assured by various travellers.

The only thing of any great interest I saw was the view of the burning mountain, Asamayama, which we gained just before reaching Oiwaké, at the end of my first long day's journey. We passed many pilgrims, both men and women, clothed in white, on their way to ascend this "holy mountain."

A dull stony road brought us next day within seven miles of Wada. Here, certainly, some fine views were to be had after crossing a bridge of boats until the village of Wada was reached, but even here I saw nothing to compare for beauty with many of the places already seen.

The third day's journey proved the most disappointing of all. A long weary road, stony and jolting, lumpy green hills covered with scrub, brought us over the Wadatoge Pass, and

in time to Lake Suwa, where I looked in vain for the
much vaunted beauties I had been led to expect. Suwa is a
circular lake, about five miles in diameter. One half of the
circle incloses flat rice fields; on the other half, low lumpy
hills rise above the water's edge.

Altogether it was by far the least interesting expedition in
Japan, and had entailed a week of solitude (for we never saw a
European until I got back to Yokohama), much expense, and
still more discomfort and hard work.

With all my heart I wish that I had been less enterprising,
and had returned quietly to Yokohama with my friend!

On the other hand, had I done so, I should doubtless have
considered that I had lost my chance of seeing the most
beautiful part of Japan.

As the man said, when assured that "zoedone" was far
better than champagne, "Well, champagne is good enough
for me." So I felt, after the weary pilgrimage to Lake Suwa
and back, that Haruna, the Aseo Pass, and Chiusengi Lake,
were "quite good enough for me."

As a rule, I think, going off the beaten track is apt to
prove a disappointment. It sounds delightful, and suggests
infinite possibilities, but the best in scenery is soon discovered
in these days of universal travel. In nine cases out of ten,
therefore, going off the beaten track now means greater
discomfort, extortionate prices, owing to monopoly and absence
of competition, and not very much to repay one when all is
said and done. I have already said so much about the fleas
in Japan, that it is needless to pile up the agony further

than by remarking the fact, that the finest and most numerous specimens haunt the tea-houses of the Nakasendo road, between Tokio and Lake Suwa.

The only interest about the latter place was a visit I paid to a large silk factory here, where more than two hundred girls are employed. On the way to the lake we had passed horses and mules, with paniers packed with baskets full of silkworm cocoons being taken to this manufactory.

The silk is wound by machinery here. The worms themselves are dried and eaten as a great luxury by the inhabitants. The smell was quite enough for me, and I was glad to hurry out of the establishment as quickly as possible. I had to retrace my steps by the same road to Itsuka and Yokohama, and felt much relieved and delighted to rejoin my friend at the latter place, after all the fatigues and isolation of the long week, during which I had been thrown entirely upon Fuji's very limited stock of English for companionship.

The proper and politic thing would have been to declare on my return that this was by far the best part of the whole trip, but an awkward habit of blurting out the truth on all occasions deprived me of even this small consolation.

I can only trust that my experience may serve as a warning to others; whilst for myself it is only philosophical to remember that one week of discomfort and disappointment was more than compensated for by the weeks of great delight and thorough enjoyment of the most beautiful country in the world.

My advice to those who are "thinking about going to Japan" is, "Don't *think*, but GO NOW."

Each year will take away something more of its originality and charm.

The rapid strides of civilization that make the country more interesting every year from *one* point of view, destroy its interest from the historical and artistic stand-point.

It is much to be feared that "civilized Christianity" may bring the usual evils in its train, and that the kindly, simple-minded, joyous little Japs may become as grasping and selfish in their dealings with each other as other civilized " Christian " men and women have too often proved themselves in these days of fierce competition. "Get to the top of the ladder yourself, and then kick it down," seems too often the modern rendering of St. Paul's maxim, " Look not every man on his own things, but every man also on the things of others."

At present this Christian virtue *is* to be found, and to be found very conspicuously, amongst this simple happy people; but it is impossible to say how long it may be so in the face of advancing civilization.

So I would say to every one; "By all means go and see them whilst they still retain some vestiges of heathen virtue, and are kind and helpful to one another." This and their happy *insouciance*, and the charm, beauty, and sunshine of the country, will make the traveller forget for a time the cold, stiff formalities of life that probably await him when he leaves this Paradise, and the gates swing back behind him.

CHAPTER VII.

A TRIP TO ALASKA.

From Yokohama to Vancouver—Fog and mist—Harmonious company—
A Tower of Babel—A stump road in Vancouver—We start for Alaska
—A few suggestions to the Pacific Coast S.S. Company—A kindly
captain—Departure Bay—An intrepid globe-trotter—Mr. Duncan's
mission—Doctor Doane's hymns—A breach of promise case—Sentiment and dollars—Salmon catching—Fort Wrangle—Fish traps—An
Indian war-dance—Totem poles—Our first glaciers—Juneau—Indian
baskets—An Indian village—The Treadwell Mine—A new play-
fellow—A female victim—Chilcote and Pyramid Harbour—The
glories of Glacier bay—A run on the glacier—We lose our way—
Suspense—All's well that ends well—Sitka—The Castle—Lady
Franklin—The ghost of the Castle—A romantic story—Mission
homes a Sitka—Presbyterian theology—A distressed teacher—
A theological distinction—A mournful exhibition—A simple prayer
—A hot saloon—A martyr to soap and water—The Greek Church
at Sitka—Peril Pass—Rolling powers of the *G. W. Elder*—Jonah
and the whale—A deserted village—Back to Victoria—Driard Hotel
—General remarks on Alaska expedition.

A TRIP to Alaska had been an old cherished plan of ours
since our visit to Victoria in Vancouver's Island some
years previously, when we had watched with envious eyes
our fellow passengers from San Francisco who were about
to embark on this expedition.

We wrote therefore beforehand for accommodation in the

steamer which was to take up passengers from Victoria on the 13th of August.

Meanwhile we had the sixteen days' voyage between Japan and Vancouver still before us, and set sail in an old Cunarder the *Abyssinia*, chartered by the Canadian Pacific Company, and leaving Yokohama on July 24th, reached the small new township of Vancouver on the morning of August 8th. A new line of steamers will shortly be built for this voyage, which will then become part of the high road between England and Japan. It is calculated that with new and powerful engines the transit can be effected in ten days.

The Canadian Pacific Railway Company's trains hope to reach Montreal from Vancouver in four or five days at the outside, and seven or eight days across the Atlantic will put Japan within little more than three weeks' journey of us, whereas at present the most direct steamer cannot take us there under forty-two days. We had a fairly smooth but a most monotonous voyage to Vancouver, scarcely seeing the sun from shore to shore.

Fog and mist accompanied us the whole way, and the dismal toll of the fog bell would have been most depressing under ordinary circumstances.

Fortunately our fellow passengers although few in number (some eighteen all told) made up in quality for lack of quantity, and we were a most harmonious company in spite of the drawback of differences of language, for many nationalities were represented amongst us—English

Australian, French, Dutch, American, Canadian, and
German. There is a very beautiful bit of scenery passed
in approaching Vancouver, namely the "Active Pass," so
called on account of the strength of the currents here
encountered. It lasts for about twenty minutes, and the
scenery is very lovely. It was our fortune to pass no less
than four times through it altogether, but we never quite
lost the first thrill of admiration which came when we first
entered the Pass, and saw the exquisite verdure-clad hills
bathed in the evening sunshine, after our long spell of
darkness and fog.

Vancouver, which lies on the mainland and is the western
terminus of the Canadian Pacific Railway, is quite a small
township, only two years old at the time of our visit, 1888.
The first town was destroyed by fire within a few months of
its existence.

The present one is a dusty, ugly little township, little
more than a mere clearing in the woods, but the harbour is
very beautiful; some large stores are springing up day by
day; there is already a fine handsome hotel built by the
Company, and Western enterprise will, doubtless, shortly
develop the little town into quite a considerable city.
Its position, as a terminus of the railway and a seaport, is
bound to bring it conspicuously to the front as the passenger
and commercial trade of the Canadian Pacific Railway
develops.

We went for a nine miles' drive over a "stump road"
in the afternoon, to see some very grand specimens of

the pine-tree to be found here, and the woods are most picturesque and beautiful.

Most of our fellow passengers were leaving next morning by the direct rail for the East, but we had to retrace our steps, and take a local steamer for Victoria, Vancouver's Island, there to await our steamer for Alaska, which started from Portland (Oregon), and was advertised to pick up passengers at Seattle, Port Townsend, and Victoria.

We had plenty of time to renew our acquaintance with the beauties of Victoria, for the Alaska steamer was two days late, owing to the amount of freight to be taken up. At length, in the early morning of Wednesday, August 15th, we drove down to the wharf, where we had landed two years previously, from San Francisco, and found our steamer, the *G. W. Elder*, alongside, and waiting for us all to embark.

On the principle of getting over disagreeables as quickly as possible, I had better at once say, that the accommodation on board the Alaska steamers leaves a great deal to be desired.

I have nothing but kindly words to speak of the captain and officers, and their wish that all should be comfortable and happy, and I am perfectly aware of the great difficulties of providing for a large number of people in these out-of-the-way parts of the world.

As Doctor Johnson remarked about a woman's preaching; "It is like a dog dancing. It is not a question as to whether the dog dances *well*, madam. The marvel is that he should dance at all!"

And so perhaps I may be called unreasonable for making

any criticism in face of the fact that, steamers do go to northerly regions, and are prepared to convey and feed those tourists who can bear "roughing it."

If I say something on the subject, it is done in no cavilling spirit, but in the real interests of the company (Pacific Coast Steam Ship) which runs these steamers, and because I am sure that a little management, and a small present sacrifice of gain, would amply repay them in the end, and make a pleasurable excursion out of what is at present a real source of miserable discomfort for most of the passengers.

People will always be found ready to "write up" *any* excursion, and perhaps some few who are exceptionally strong and exceptionally thick-skinned may really believe something of what they write.

But I am sure that if our hundred and twenty passengers had been asked, and *had spoken the truth* without fear or favour, seven-eighths of them would have admitted the truth of what I am about to say.

The *G. W. Elder* is a 1,200 ton freight steamer, and in no way fitted to carry passengers unless the numbers were reduced very much below the figure on the occasion of our excursion.

The cabins are extremely small, and when three passengers are packed in each cabin, like herrings in a barrel, it is easily understood that there must be considerable drawbacks to a purely pleasure excursion.

One does not so much resent overcrowding when a steamer is merely used as a necessary evil and mode of conveyance from one part of the world to another. Moreover, I have never before travelled in a steamer where the cabin accommodation was so limited.

It is only fair to say that larger and better appointed steamers were put on by the company for a year or two, and taken off because they did not pay.

This, however, seems to me to have been short-sighted policy. To utilize a freight boat for a pleasure excursion is doubtless a temporary economy, but with the vast Continent of America at hand as patrons, I cannot believe that the company would not have recouped itself over and over again for the extra comfort afforded, had they "possessed their souls in patience" for a year or two, and been content to sink a little capital until the expedition should be more widely advertised.

Allowing however that this experiment cannot be repeated at present, I think much might be done by reducing the number of passengers for each trip.

I suppose the answer will be, that "the proof of the pudding is in the eating," and so long as people do not object to being flattened like pancakes and undressing on their berths for lack of room, the company would be foolish and quixotic to make other arrangements for them.

The question is, will people *continue* to eat the pudding? Doubtless the steamers at present are crowded, but then Alaska just now is a novelty.

I cannot believe that this Spartan endurance will continue in the future when the novelty of the thing has worn off a little.

Then, again, as to the question of food.

Many would have been content (as we should have been) with the very simplest fare, decently cooked and served. As it was, food, good in itself and in unnecessary quantities, became uneatable from the manner in which it was presented to us. Each meal had to be duplicated to meet the requirements of so many. All the food was, however, cooked at one time, and left to get cold between the first and second dinners; and one day at luncheon alone, I counted thirty different dishes lying about and tumbling over each other, all half cold, greasy, and unappetizing.

Two or three well-cooked courses—say, soup, meat, and a choice of vegetables and puddings—would have satisfied any reasonable person on such an expedition, and if served hot at each dinner would have given far more satisfaction and comfort than these endless dishes of ill-cooked viands.

Even the phlegmatic Yankees began "to kick" after the first few days, but so few people have the moral courage to tell the truth! No one likes "to make himself disagreeable." Each one thinks, "Well, it won't matter to me. When this voyage is over I am not likely to come again," and so the evil grows unchecked. The purser assured me that no one had ever grumbled or expressed the slightest dissatisfaction before myself, and it may be true. I can only say that plenty of dissatisfaction was expressed behind his back, and I think it is unfair both to the company and the officers, not to be outspoken;

especially when so much of the evil can be so easily remedied by a little supervision and management.

Our Captain (Hunter) was a most delightful man, and a universal favourite; always genial, always in good spirits, and ready to help every one to the very utmost, and make us all have as "good a time" as lay in *his* power.

We steamed up the first day from Victoria to a pretty harbour called "Departure Bay," on the *lucus à non lucendo* principle, for there we stuck at the side of a coal wharf from Wednesday at 7 P.M. till 10 A.M. on the following Friday.

The delay was occasioned by our having to take in coal, which had not even been quarried until our arrival.

A telegram was said to have been sent on four days ahead for it, but apparently with little effect. I believe some disagreement between the coal agents was at the bottom of the *contretemps*, but we poor victims were sorry not to have had the chance of joining the vessel two days later, by rail from Victoria, which could easily have been done.

The heat was intense when we landed, and attempted to sit among the trees on shore, and we were fain to return to the ship, and get through the time as best we could.

Nearly all the passengers were Americans, and very pleasant and friendly some of them were! An energetic American lady who had left a complaisant husband in New York, whilst she went round the world alone, interested me as much as any one, especially by the ingenuity with which she had planned to make the lengthy excursion without any trunk or baggage. Two diminutive Russia leather hand-bags and a "strap" to hold wraps, contained her modest wardrobe. What a splendid campaigner she would have made!

The old joke of the *Saturday Review* about the lady who went "through the Pyrenees with two petticoats" pales before this far more wonderful achievement. She had been six weeks *en route* when we met her, and her one hat and single pair of boots were not as yet much the worse for wear. Of course no curios could be bought on the way except such as could be shipped off at once to New York, to await her return.

Leaving Departure Bay on a wet, foggy morning, we steamed off, to the general delight, although for some hours little could be seen except the enveloping clouds.

After passing the Gulf of Georgia, Johnstone's Straits, and Queen Charlotte's Sound, we found ourselves opposite Princess Royal Island, and a neat little white Indian village with European looking houses, called "Bella Bella," and also one or two waterfalls, which seemed very small to us, fresh from our Japanese experiences.

Next morning it was interesting to arrive at a place formerly called Port Chester, but now re-christened "Metakahtla" by Mr. Duncan, the Scotch missionary, who had settled down here only a year ago with an Indian tribe.

This latter inhabited a place of the same name in British Columbia, but were turned out by the British Government.

They would have been allowed to remain on sufferance, but deprived of all their rights, and forced to attend an Episcopalian form of worship.

There was, moreover, a dispute about their land, which Mr. Duncan says might have been decided in their favour had they been able to afford to go to law. Whatever the rights of the case may be, they were packed off here under his charge, and have made a clearing and established a settlement, running up a number of wooden houses.

A long building running out on wooden stakes into the water at present serves as a church, but will eventually be turned into a salmon tinning establishment. We landed here and heard part of an Indian service. The Indians here are perfectly civilized, and looked very bright and intelligent.

It was hard to believe that they were pure " Indian," for some of the children were scarcely coloured at all, and all of them looked more like half-breeds.

They belong to the Tsimpean tribe (pronounced soft, like Shimchean). The tribe consists of 800 in all, but many of the men were off to the fisheries just then. There are 170 children entered on the books of the day school and Sunday school.

They sang some hymns very prettily, but in English, not being able to translate our English words into their many-syllabled language.

A kindly and pleasant Dr. Doane, who was on board our steamer with his wife and two neat little daughters, turned out to be the author of several of Moody and Sankey's hymn tunes.

Amongst others, he wrote the music for "Safe in the Arms of Jesus," and the world famed "Old, old Story." The Indian children sang several of these hymns, much to his delight.

Certainly the clean, happy, civilized look of these Indians speaks volumes for Mr. Duncan's labours amongst them.

One can hardly believe that the settlement is only a year old, and yet our Captain brought this missionary up here just a year before our visit to his settlement.

All his supplies are carried up by steamer from Portland.

It seems a curiously isolated life, for there are only two white men in the settlement, but Mr. Duncan looks very well and happy, and has a bright rosy face, which made one fervently trust for his sake that the tribe might never relapse into cannibal ways!

The European dress, as usual, is most disfiguring to the Indians. They look, as the Japs did, sloppy and untidy, instead of dignified and comfortable, as they would have done in their own picturesque costume.

Leaving Mr. Duncan with many hearty good wishes, as well as more substantial assurance of our interest in his great work, we steamed on for two or three hours further to Fort Tongas, where another stop was made.

My circumnavigating American lady friend amused me very much that evening by a story of an English friend of hers, who fell desperately in love with an American gentleman in New York, at the mature age of forty-five. I grieve to say that the American jilted her, whereupon the tough spinster brought a breach of promise case against him, and refused to give up his letters under $5,000, which were duly paid over to her by his solicitors.

" How that woman loved that man, to be sure," murmured my informant, " and then to think how she was cheated ! Why, she never saw more than $3,500, for her lawyer kept the rest for his expenses. Ah ! Englishwomen are always bad at business ! "

The mixture of love, romance, and the almighty dollar struck me as very funny.

On Sunday evening we stopped at " Tongas Narrows," at a " salmon cannery," to discharge a freight of tin sheeting to be used for making salmon tins.

The ship does not now go right up to Fort Tongas, for the navigation is considered too dangerous.

Great excitement prevailed amongst us. The rain was coming down in a perfect deluge, but just across, on the mainland, were a few cottages and a waterfall at the back, from which a stream ran down to the sea. Up this stream hundreds and thousands of salmon were to be seen leaping and dancing about—so numerous that the men of the party caught them in their hands and threw them on shore. As one man said, " You could scarcely see the water for the salmon ! "

The fish only averaged from five to seven pounds in weight, but the quantity was marvellous. Of course there was no question of *sport*, only the excitement of such a novel scene, and of watching the enormous leaps made right up the waterfall by the poor salmon in their attempts to escape from their capturers.

One of our most devout fellow passengers of the afternoon at " Metakahtla," became just as enthusiastic over the salmon as he had been earlier in the day over the Psalter; a striking example of the undoubted fact that temperament has much to do with our special religious development.

Next day we were glad to get out all the winter clothing we had brought with us, for the cold weather had fairly set in, and would continue now until our return to Victoria, as our course would be constantly in a north-westerly direction.

We landed shortly at Fort Wrangle, a township with two small churches and a number of tiny wooden houses, looking extremely European, as all these Alaska Indian villages do.

The true Alaska Indians are of the Kleinket (pronounced *Klinket*) tribes, Mr. Duncan's settlement being an exception, and having migrated here from British Columbia.

A low line of blue mountains surrounds Fort Wrangle, but the fog and mist lay deep upon them. The vegetation is bleak and scrubby, endless small fir trees lining the banks and covering the small islands which are passed from time to time.

There is very little of interest to be bought in these Indian villages. The Indians stand out for their money, asking exorbitant prices and having a perfect monopoly in these far away regions where no healthy breath of competition can enter.

They are spoiled by the periodical inroads of travellers coming up on the summer steamers, who outbuy and *outvie* one another and so run up the prices. In the eagerness of getting anything at all where the choice is so limited, one is apt to forget to ask oneself if the article in question is really worth having.

Some curious wooden traps for catching halibut (fish) struck me as more characteristic than anything else ; for the silver bracelets are dear and by no means pretty or curious.

These traps are very simply made, merely two pieces of wood joined together at an angle, and a steel hook inside. The bait is placed near the junction of the wood, and the fish, after taking it, gets hooked in trying to " back out " again. In the original old Indian traps these hooks are always made of whales' teeth ; the steel hook being an innovation.

Many of the Indian women here wear a piece of ivory inserted in the *chin*, a curious and disagreeable custom. It looks just like a tooth protruding through the chin. They remove these bits of ivory as one would an earring and slip them back again from the inside of the mouth. The women begin to wear these ornaments when very young, increasing the size of the ivory as they grow older.

The Alaska Indians are only slightly coloured, and look less fierce than the North American ones that I have seen. No doubt they could show fight on occasion, but compared with the latter they are rendered more helpless from depending entirely on their canoes, whereas the prairie Indians have "all the world before them where to roam."

We saw a very amusing Indian war dance in a shed at Fort Wrangle. One Indian beat the drum, and two others came in, dressed up with feathers sticking out of their heads. One man had his head covered with a coloured flax cap, matching a sort of apron or blanket, worn after the fashion of a kilt, and made of coloured wools. The second man wore an apron ornamented by a double row of bears' claws, and held in his hands two tambourines, made of circles of wood with bears' claws hanging from them by coloured wools. These tambourines he clanged together during the whole performance.

A gentleman of our party afterwards bought both the drum and cymbals, for twenty-seven dollars.

The dance continued for about half an hour, ending by one warrior tumbling down and making a very good "stage death" on the floor, and then reviving to spring, dance and shout at his adversary, till finally the whole performance ended by a war whoop of intense shrillness, and a general stampede and collapse of all three men who had taken part in it. They shouted out in English "All over," "Goodbye!" and we took the hint and retired, having paid twenty-five cents each for a dance that was decidedly far more characteristic, and less of a swindle than most of the native dances in other parts of the world.

Fort Wrangle is noted for the number of curious "totem poles" to be found here in front of the native houses. These poles are made by cutting down a tree and setting it up in front of the house, carved with all manner of quaint figures of men and animals. It seems to serve partly as an historical and genealogical "family tree," and is also connected with native superstition, and supposed to keep off evil spirits. Some of these carvings are very clever, as well as curious, especially in one case, where the marks of a bear's feet had been carved up the tree, to the very top, where sat an image of the bear himself, carved out of the wood and crouched up in a most extraordinary attitude, with a beaming sort of leer upon his wide open mouth. A wolf, with a head like a crocodile, and legs like a frog, whales, owls, crows, frogs, and now and then a human face—all these were represented in turn, tier upon tier, on these curious poles.

It seemed very inconsistent to see two very ancient totem poles set up in front of a modern looking wooden house, with two bay windows! Many of the houses here have been shut up and deserted. No wonder! for it is one of the dreariest looking spots I ever beheld!

After lunch we went up on the bridge of the steamer to see the glaciers in the neighbourhood of Wrangle as we steamed on towards Junean, the chief trading port in Alaska.

The glaciers were certainly the best thing we had yet seen. Very weird and desolate the scenery looked, but we counted eight glaciers all ahead of us and around us at the same time, some of them coming sheer down to the water's edge, where a quantity of drift ice lay around its margin.

The difficulty is to realize that this water is all *salt* water, and that the glaciers are formed from 1,200 to 3,000 feet only above the sea line, for we had not as yet passed any mountains loftier than this. Moreover, we were only at 57° of latitude, a little above the most northerly part of Scotland.

One curious looking rock, rising up close to a glacier here, is called the Devil's Thumb.

The cold was intense as we steamed through all this glacier district, and standing on the bridge was by no means an unmixed pleasure in such biting winds, but having come so far and gone through so much discomfort, it seemed folly not to take advantage of any possible compensation in the way of sight-seeing.

We reached Junean at midnight of Monday (August 21st), and were tethered all night at a noisy wharf. In the morning we watched the poor sheep and cows being landed by the simple process of throwing them over the side of the ship to swim to land as they best could. Some vainly tried to return to the steamer, but were driven back. Two sheep, however, becoming hopelessly frightened, the men had to let down a boat and row with them to the shore.

Junean is backed by high hills, and built on a small plateau just at their foot and close on to the bay. It was very cloudy when we first landed, but cleared off by degrees, and then the town looked very picturesque in situation. Still, it is cold and desolate even at this time of year, and it seemed to me that a little bride of eighteen, who had come up with us, would require a good deal of affection to reconcile her to a residence here of some years at least with her husband, who has a large store in the village.

The European portion of the little township lies nearest the wharf, and here also are the curio shops where goods are sold at rather exorbitant prices. Some native blankets, made from the wool of the mountain sheep, fetched fifty dollars each. They were small, but the colouring was very good, being a mixture of blue, yellow, and black, with a long white fringe all round. Coloured baskets made of plaited fibre, taken from between the bark and the tree, are the chief speciality of Juneau, and these are both useful and pretty, being very supple and easily packed.

No compression hurts them, for the shape is easily restored by a little water, and they can be utilized as work or waste paper baskets, the colouring being generally very artistic and pretty. After making our purchases, we walked over the hill to a pretty looking Indian village on the beach on the other side.

Very picturesque this village looked, seen from the enchanting distance of the hill, but it was filthily dirty upon further acquaintance.

Some canoes lay on the shore, dirty old women in coloured blankets and still dirtier children squatted around, and the air was redolent of stale fish and grease and other abominations.

Many of the women smear their faces all over with a sort of greasy coal black, giving the effect of a mask, for the natural faces of these Indians (the Auk tribe) is barely copper coloured, being more the shade of a rather swarthy European.

The Indian native houses here are arranged in the following fashion : three or four tiers of wooden steps run round the four sides of the house, and all the cooking utensils, clothing, &c., lie upon these, as also do most of the inhabitants ; three or four families occupying the same house. Some children are generally playing about on the earthen floor, and in the middle a large square is cleared and slightly sunken, to make the fire-place—a very simple one.

The Indians merely kindle a large wood fire in the centre of the floor, and cook their food there, four large poles with beams across marking it out and being utilized for smoking the fish which hangs in large quantities from the poles.

We then walked on to see the place where these Indians cremate their dead.

Several large wooden mausoleums with native blankets nailed in front and wooden crosses at the top, marked the spot. A window in front of such a wooden "tomb" enabled us to see some common American wooden trunks inside, piled one on the top of the other, in which the ashes of the departed are kept !

It seemed a strangely incongruous idea when compared with the beautifully carved and ornamented vases of the ancients—to descend to a *Saratoga trunk !* Some gaudy handkerchiefs hung like banners from the roof.

In the afternoon we steamed off to Port Douglas, nearly opposite Junean, where the famous Treadwell gold mine is located.

We visited here first the stamping mill, where, amidst

deafening noise, innumerable great crushers are at work, crushing out the stony quartz.

This is reduced to powder, and washed through over large troughs, into other troughs with a constant *sideward* motion which sieves the quartz water. Then the gold (free gold) being heaviest, falls into a receiver, as at the "placer" mines in America, and the rest, containing the lighter sulphate of gold and gold pyrites, is conveyed further on, to be dealt with by a new chemical process which frees it from the rest of the diluted quartz. Even the free gold (or true gold) has to be separated later from the earth surrounding it, but its greater weight causes it to free itself by dropping away from the general mass.

In this mill no one could either speak or hear. It seemed as if one would never be able to hear again; and the most ludicrous dumb show went on, every one trying to point out and explain, and no one being able to speak when it came to the test, for the noise was so deafening that it was impossible even to pitch the voice.

This stamping-mill, the largest in the world, has two hundred and forty stamping machines at work, and crushes from 800 to 1,000 tons of quartz daily.

From hence we climbed up a very steep hill to see the quarry from which the quartz is taken, for this famous mine is a "superficial" one, that is to say, it is worked from the outside by blasting the rocks on the hill side, which are full of gold quartz. The gold is not found in any great quantities at any special point, but the whole mass of the quartz is so impregnated with it that it pays to work it out by this new and economical chemical process. The average yield, however, is not more than nine to twelve dollars' worth of gold to the ton.

A deep fissure has been blasted in the rocks, leaving a large circular pit, about three hundred feet deep from the top of the cliff. A shaft is sunk from the cliff-top to the circular pit, and thence further down to the level of the sea, where a tunnel conveys the quartz to the crushing-mill.

On the side of this rocky ravine holes are drilled to receive gunpowder for the blasting which takes place twice a day. It is the largest gold mine in this part of the world, and most interesting, as all the operations can be so easily seen.

As we returned to the ship after seeing this mine, we found a boy on the wharf holding a dear little baby bear of four months old by a chain. A gentleman and his wife from the Eastern States had promised their little boy, a child of four years old, to look out for a "real bear" when they started upon this expedition.

The opportunity was too good to be lost. The bear was bought for a few dollars and speedily transferred to the upper deck, where he became a great favourite, but began by giving rather a severe *pat* with his paw to one of three little pups belonging to the captain, who were already established there.

It was a very tame little bear, but evidently did not wish to make acquaintance with any "inferior animals," although quite friendly with the human ones on board !

Quite early next morning, about 5 A.M., I chanced to look out of my port window, and saw a glacier we were passing which came sheer down to the water's edge, with a very thin line of fir trees between it and the sea.

The previous evening we had watched a glorious sunset from the deck, which lighted up the Juncan mountains with shades of faint green, crimson and gold, whilst a lovely deep rose pink covered the glacier close at hand.

We arrived at Pyramid Harbour, close to Chilcote, at 6.30 A.M. It is so named after a small mound of earth in pyramid form at the mouth of the harbour. Snow mountains rise up all around, and several glaciers are to be seen within seven or eight miles. This is merely a salmon canning depot, but one poor lady who came up with us has to live here for the summer months, as her husband has an interest in the large canning establishment. She pointed out to me a tiny log house with no windows which is to be her abode. Yet she seemed a refined fragile woman. I cannot understand any *American* woman submitting to such a dismal fate!

We went out in a small launch to see the salmon nets, and to bring back a " take " of four hundred and fifty salmon, varying from five to twelve pounds in weight. It was horrible to see the men hooking the poor creatures whilst still alive, to shift them from one part of the boat to the other, throwing back the worthless ones into the sea. A most brutalizing occupation I should think! It was a relief to look from the blood red water up at the beautiful snow-tipped mountains and glaciers.

I have omitted to mention an adventure after leaving the Treadwell mine the previous evening. After steaming for about an hour, the engines were suddenly reversed, and I found that we were retracing our steps at about ten o'clock at night. It turned out that the chief engineer and a priest had been suddenly found missing!

They had gone back to the mine, thinking that we should not sail till midnight, whereas the captain found he could get off after discharging his freight, by nine o'clock.

The discovery of their absence was made by the merest chance from the lucky fact that something was required which the chief engineer had in charge. Of course, a half-hour whistle had been sounded, but the men, being in the mine, had failed to hear this, and their plight would have been a miserable one had the discovery not been made till next morning.

We left Pyramid Harbour and Chilcote within a few hours of our arrival there, and steaming off to Glacier Bay, the most northerly point of the expedition, cast anchor there next morning (August 23rd) at 10 A.M.

What marvels met our delighted eyes! I think this one spot repays one for the whole expedition, and puts to flight once and for ever, any comparison with Norway, Switzerland, or any other part of the snow-clad regions which I have ever visited.

Walls or cliffs of ice, 320 feet, sheer down to the water

and of every exquisite shade of deep and faint green and blue face one as the bay is entered. The Muir glacier (which we ascended later) seemed quite close upon us for miles before we came to anchor.

There is one wide expanse of bay, surrounded by grand snow mountains, with glaciers running sheer down to the sea, and extending over limitless fields of snow and ice for forty miles and more! The highest mountain peaks lay to our left as the bay was entered.

Mount Carillon is 15,900 feet high, Fairweather 14,000, and La Perouse also 14,000 feet high. The face of the Muir glacier is like a frozen "Horse Shoe Fall," only that these icy walls are more than twice the height of Niagara, and with the brilliant sun shining full upon them the effect was like fairyland.

I forgave Alaska all its bad weather, the biting winds and driving rain we had encountered so many days, in consideration of this one gloriously beautiful day at the very culminating point of the whole expedition.

We had passed numbers of small icebergs, and several fairly large ones, but none quite to compare with those we had seen *en route* for Quebec.

A great quantity of drift-ice lay about, requiring careful navigation as we wound our way through it to our anchorage for the day. The boats took us on shore, and there we wandered up a very steep gully, and then for nearly two miles over a very rough "moraine," to get on to the glacier proper, and thence climbed upwards to a point where a glorious view met our eyes.

Here a flagstaff is planted, and a book kept in a wooden box, so that adventurous travellers may inscribe their names. Here, also, the glacier expedition is supposed to end, but the spirit of the place was too much for me. After actually turning towards home, and in spite of a very heavy influenza cold, it seemed as if one *could* not leave it. With little difficulty I persuaded my friend to return, and she and I struck out a path for ourselves over the ice in a different direction, and just under the snow mountains, which form a crescent around this immense glacier, which is a mile and a half wide, and forty miles in length, and said to be the largest in the world.

We counted eight distinct glaciers as we stood upon this one, and backing them, the crescent of snow clad mountains, an exquisite palest blue sky beyond, and a haze on the mountains which melted into the blue of the sky until we could scarcely see where snow ended and the sky line began.

We were entranced by the weird beauty of the scene and the sort of *warm desolation* about it, for the colouring was far from cold, and yet one had such a "*north poley*" feeling of being at the very ends of the earth.

As we stood, a sound like distant artillery came over the glacier every now and again as huge pieces of the ice fell with loud splashes into the sea.

It is said that the water here is salt below and fresh above, owing no doubt to the number of icebergs which are continually melting into the latter.

We spent more than three hours on the glacier, returning

by a new route, and nearly losing our way, which made me very nervous, for the captain had said he would remain only four hours, and one o'clock, the limit, had already arrived. I thought to myself, "Suppose the half-hour whistle sounded *now*, when we do not in the least know how to get back, what should we do?"

We could not "coo-ee," for the voices would not carry, and amongst so many passengers we should not be missed until dinner time, if even then, for the hasty "double scramble" was very unlike the usual orderly ship's dinner, where each one has his or her appointed place.

In any case, the ship would be four hours on her way by that time, and even nine or ten hours of cold and hunger was no pleasing prospect.

I did not dare to mention these fears to my friend, for by this time we were both getting pretty well exhausted by the long and apparently endless scramble over boulders of rock and ice and snow which tripped us up from time to time.

In fact we both became so suspiciously cheerful and so very sure that the next hundred yards or so *must* bring us within sight of the ship that I felt convinced that the same horrible idea was passing through my companion's mind and that we were both remembering the adventure of the chief engineer and the priest.

How horribly frightened they had looked when they came on board that night! And yet their fate would have been a Paradise compared with ours, for I think we must have perished with cold and hunger, even in a few hours, on this ice-bound spot.

It was real terror for a time, and I wished with all my heart that we had returned quietly with most of the passengers; but my friend and I said never a word to each other of any possible disaster until at long, long last, the funnels of the *G. W. Elder* came in sight. I shall never forget the relief of that moment! Of course in this case our own rashness was to blame entirely; but I do think, on such an out-of-the-world expedition, where being left behind probably means starvation and death, it would be well to adopt the extra precaution of a "roll call" before each fresh start.

It is too much to expect that the captain, however clever and observing, can always be absolutely sure that each one of a hundred and twenty or hundred and thirty passengers, has returned to the ship.

However, all is well that ends well! If we were foolhardy, "*nous en étions quittes par la peur*," and Glacier Bay will remain till the last day of my life as one of the grandest and most unrivalled sights in memory's picture gallery.

Steaming away from this magnificent spot, we passed slowly out of range of the grand snow mountains, into a very different but equally beautiful scene, entering Idaho Inlet.

This is an exquisite inlet of the sea, surrounded by verdure clad mountains. The lovely sunset reflections, and a few white gulls skimming over the glass-like waters formed a very charming and restful picture after the grander but scarcely more beautiful scenes of the morning. Next morning we were up in good time to watch the approach to Sitka, the capital of Alaska.

Sitka is by far the most beautifully situated of all the Alaska towns, as it is also the cleanest and most civilized looking.

The town is surrounded by lovely mountains, a few of which have snow on their highest peaks.

A grand extinct volcanic mountain, named by Captain Cook, Mount Edgcombe, reminded me by its sweeping lines of Fuji-yama in Japan, only on a very small scale.

Sitka is a much smaller township than I had pictured for the capital of Alaska—just a line of white houses along the shore form the Indian portion of it. A piece of reserved ground with small cannon, used as a drill ground, divides this from the European portion, which is chiefly occupied by American official residences and an old tumble-down wooden " castle."

The latter is a remnant of the Russian occupation, but it looks more like an ordinary wooden house than *our* idea of a " castle," the walls and the steps up to it falling alike into swift decay.

We climbed up the mouldering wooden steps to a little tower which commands a glorious view over Sitka and the lovely bay, dotted all over with green islands.

Uninteresting as it looks, the Sitka castle has two most interesting associations. In the first place, Lady Franklin occupied two rooms here for some months when she accompanied the exploring expedition in search of her husband. Secondly, there is a ghost-story connected with the building.

Many years ago, during the time of the Russian occupation, a governor of the castle (Baranoff I think was the name) lived here with his niece, a very beautiful girl, who was beloved by, and herself in love with, a young Russian officer. Not being "noble," the latter was considered beneath her in rank, and the governor, to stop any risk of an elopement, managed to have the young man sent off on a wild expedition to quell a disturbance amongst the Indians—such warlike raids being common enough in those days, when the Indian tribes were still very powerful. Meanwhile, a Russian noble came to stay with the governor, in every way a suitable match for the girl, and her uncle insisted upon her marrying him. The poor girl, though faithful at heart to her lover, was too weak and too much frightened to resist the pressure brought to bear upon her. The marriage was hastened on, and took place amidst great rejoicings, and a grand banquet was given in a long room which commands a lovely view of Sitka Bay, and which we had specially remarked whilst wandering over the castle.

Meanwhile the first lover "had got wind of the affair," and managed to throw up his command and return secretly to Sitka.

He concealed himself in the precincts of the castle, and at a critical moment during the banquet, when the bride's health was about to be drunk, he rushed in and stabbed her to the heart, throwing himself out of the window immediately afterwards, to be picked up a senseless corpse!

It is said that his spirit haunts the castle, and that once a year, in the month of December, a light is seen there, and the figure becomes visible to those who are brave enough to face "the ghost."

We had expected to find many curiosities in the Indian village at Sitka, but were woefully disappointed.

There were no native blankets to be had, and the bracelets and baskets were dearer, and not so good as those we had despised at Junean, being told to keep our money till we reached Sitka and found a greater choice there.

After dinner my friend and I strolled along the shore of the upper town towards the Presbyterian Mission houses.

There are two of these, one for boys and one for girls, under the charge of Mr. Austin, a pleasant, genial man. They are almost exclusively devoted to Indian children, who board and live in the respective houses, having nice wooden bedsteads with comfortable mattresses and blankets.

There are one hundred and seventy children in all.

A nice bright little American teacher took us all over the girls' department, and professed to be much shocked at *my* being so shocked when I read part of the Westminster Catechism written up on the blackboard for the benefit of these little Indians.

"God of His mere goodwill and pleasure, having from all eternity predestined the elect to everlasting life," &c., &c.

I said to her, "Then what earthly good is it for the 'un-elected children' to make any effort at all? Why not 'have a good time' here, any way, since nothing they can do will alter their fate one way or the other?"

"Oh, you must not say that," was the feebly orthodox reply of my companion.

"But I *do* say it. Is it not the logical outcome of your belief? What else does it mean?"

"Oh, I don't know! I cannot explain it myself, but I *have* heard it explained in some way," she answered, in real distress at my heresy.

And so this immoral doctrine is daily forced down the poor little Indian throats by a teacher who has herself "*forgotten how it was explained to her!*" Mercifully, I do not suppose the children understand much of that or any other dogma or creed, and probably assimilate only the beautiful, wholesome idea of a Father, pitying and loving His children.

The little teacher herself looked far too bright and innocent to believe anything so horrible. As she was absolutely unable to give any sort of ground for holding such a belief except the fact that "*she was a Presbyterian,*" let us hope it may have fallen equally harmlessly upon the soil of *her* kindly little heart!

When I spoke rather strongly, saying, "No, I *don't* believe it. I don't pay the God I worship so poor a compliment as to believe such things of Him," she answered simply, "Ah! then you must be a Methodist."

This led to my clearing up what has puzzled me about

" Methodists " in America, ever since I heard a liberal-minded Baptist minister in Boston speak of possible redemption for the whole world.

I thought he must be a specially broad-minded man, but this young American lady told me that all American Methodists differ from Presbyterians on this one point, and uphold free will as opposed to election.

So much the better for the Methodists ! It is at least a step towards the light.

A painful performance followed this theological discussion.

We all went into the classroom whilst this poor little woman struggled to beat out a little mental arithmetic and spelling from the very dull looking Indian boys and girls under her charge.

The apparent stupidity was owing partly no doubt to nervousness, but I cannot think that they would have compared under any circumstances with American and English children. We must however remember that they have to learn everything through the medium of a foreign tongue.

It must require immense patience to deal with them. Noting the unflagging brightness, and the unwearied, sweet cheerfulness of the teacher even with the most stupid and sulky looking pupils in her charge, I wondered still more that she should give her Creator credit for so little patience and long-suffering with the creatures of His own creation.

The mournful spelling business at length came to an end, and then the children sang *Hail, Columbia !* to the tune of the *Red, White and Blue*—another cool "crib," which reminds me that one evening I went on deck and found our fellow passengers dancing what they pointed out to me with great pride as the *"real, original, old Virginian reel" our* Sir Roger de Coverley!

I annihilated them with this piece of information on the spot, saying it had been danced in England years before America was "born or thought of!" I fear this is not true! Any way we certainly did not import Sir Roger de Coverley into England from Virginia!

The evening I am describing ended by the singing of some of Dr. Doane's hymns, which he accompanied himself upon the harmonium, and then a little Indian girl prayed very simply and prettily in her broken English.

"Dear Father! Bless all these *gentlemans* and ladies that have come so far to see us, and take them safe back. Dear Father, bless Miss Kelsey [their matron] if she leaves in the ship to-morrow, and bring her safe back. Dear Father, bless all of us boys and girls here and lay Thy hand upon us, and give us thy Holy Spirit," &c.

Each sentence began "Dear Father."

It seemed somehow to take away the nauseous flavour of the Westminster Catechism extracts which still remained on the blackboard, and to leave us only the memory of this little Indian child, standing there with bent head and clasped hands, so free from all self-consciousness, talking in her pretty, childlike, trusting way, to "Our Father which art in heaven."

Many of the young Indians were away at the time of our visit to the mission, having gone up country on rafts, to bring back sufficient firewood for the long, dreary and rainy winter.

There is also a hospital in connection with this mission, a bright looking, low white wooden building just beyond the schools.

Most of the ship's crew had gone off on this evening to attend an impromptu dance given in one of the official residences, where Judge and Mrs. Keatley (the new American judge and his wife), whom we had brought up with us, were going to live.

Were my lot cast in Alaska I should certainly choose Sitka as headquarters in preference to Junean or Wrangle. Sitka is much cleaner, more civilized, and far more beautiful, but—oh ! it would be a terribly lonely and monotonous life !

Beauty of scenery alone cannot make up for the loss of nearly everything else that makes " life worth living." I think Wilkie Collins in his *Woman in White* refers to this fact—that no scenery however beautiful can alone satisfy the human heart—as a proof of our immortality. Hence our craving for something more lasting than the decaying nature around us. Finite beings ought to be content with finite surroundings when the latter are altogether beautiful. This is the gist of the argument; a very fair one I think.

During our two days' stay in Sitka a picnic to a beautiful bay was got up by the captain, in the interests of a poor girl who had sprained her foot a few days before in stepping over the gangway of the steamer, and had thus been deprived of the glorious trip to the glaciers.

It would have been a sad loss to any of us, but the misfortune was specially hard upon this young creature, who had been looking forward to it so enthusiastically, and had, moreover, provided herself with a new pair of "rubbers" for the occasion.

Many of the passengers, myself amongst the number, had by this time contracted very severe colds.

This seems to be a necessary evil, in spite of wraps and warm clothing.

The saloon becomes intolerably heated by steam and humanity combined, and going from such an atmosphere into glorious sunshine and biting winds, is pretty sure to bring on some form of cold and influenza.

My own heavy influenza, which led later to a serious illness, was caught at any rate in the cause of cleanliness, by turning out of a warm berth in a deck-cabin every morning, to make my way across the wet decks and down through the saloon to the one bath-room at the far end.

When we first went on board, this *one* bath-room was a terrible shock to our English ideas, especially as it was filled up with all the rubbish that could find no place elsewhere.

The steward looked amused at our despair when we calculated probable chances of getting a "morning tub," with a hundred and twenty-five competitors.

"Nobody ever does use the bath-room much on these trips; but if you ladies have a fancy for it, I will clear these things out and you can be called at any time you like in the mornings." This sounded too good to be true, but his prophecy was justified by events, and it absolutely turned out that my friend and I, and an old ship's captain on board, were the only three out of the hundred and twenty who ever "troubled the waters," so far as the bathroom was concerned.

Florence Nightingale has truly said, that any one can be clean who has the will and a tumbler of water, but one cannot help sometimes wondering if the tumbler of water is really utilized by those who refuse greater facilities? My friend, fortunately for her, had a saloon cabin, and so was able to exercise the virtue which ranks next to godliness with no disastrous effects.

A charming walk from Sitka takes one past the Mission Houses to the "Indian River," which flows down through a beautiful gorge into the sea at this point. To reach the spot, we walked through exquisite fern-grown, leafy woods, full of a shrub which has bold, coarse green leaves and very bright red berries in bunches. Another tree, with very dark *blue* berries, formed a striking contrast, whilst mosses and maidenhair fern abounded on every side.

The "bush" became soon too much entangled and the ground too wet for further exploration, so we re-crossed the wooden bridge that spans the river and strolled slowly back towards the Greek Church. This, with its white and green spire and two gold Greek crosses, forms a conspicuous object in the first view of Sitka.

There were some curious old pictures in this church, painted partly in oils, with the clothing, &c., added in carved silver, through which the painted portions peep; reminding one of a child's toy picture-book in which the same face serves for a succession of gay costumes. One "Madonna and Child" here has real merit, only the Madonna as usual looks as if she had been taken out of a "Book of Beauty" with her great big eyes and rosebud mouth.

I suppose it requires the genius of a Raphael to dare to paint the Virgin Mother as a peasant—but a peasant inspired !.

The Greek Bishop from San Francisco comes to visit the twelve Greek churches of Alaska once a year.

This special congregation consists of 200 members (Russian), but there are also 1,000 Indians, and they, like the Presbyterians, have their Mission Schools, but on a far larger scale.

The usual gorgeous sunset greeted us as we steamed away from Sitka, passing through the extremely narrow and dangerous path, called appropriately "Peril Pass." A pilot is necessary here, for the navigation is most intricate amongst all the islands and shallows of this inland sea. From Sitka, the steamer retraces her steps, north-west, to Juneau and thence to Fort Wrangle, but from here a slight divergence of route is made in order to deliver freight at one or two places not visited before.

Passing through Clarence Straits, on the return voyage, a

terrible storm came on, and we spent some miserable hours, having a grand opportunity of testing the rolling capacity of the *G. W. Elder.*

We had heard dark rumours before leaving Victoria that she had been re-christened the *G. W. Roller*, but it was only after this and some similar experience that I could fully appreciate the fact that this boat had to be taken off the direct San Francisco and Victoria service because no one would make the crossing in her.

When other ships on the service were carrying 200 and 300 passengers, the poor *G. W. Elder* was forced to sail with twelve or fourteen!

The rolling must certainly be a "true bill" if Captain Hunter had the ship then, for no one could wish to sail under a kinder or more obliging captain.

The rain and cold had set in again after two fine days at Sitka, and one whole day between Loring and Burrowes Bay was spent of necessity in the over-heated saloon, which a missionary and his poor over-taxed wife, three small but very noisy children, a cradle, and a perambulator, had turned by this time into a nursery *pro tem.*

This, moreover, was part of the poor woman's holiday! I think she must have been as much relieved as we were when the whole party was landed at one of the mission stations at the end of the brief outing.

Another stoppage was made at Fort Tongas, where we went on shore to see more totem poles, a really fine collection of carved bears, whales, and wolves. Two large wooden whales are carved here in a horizontal position, each one holding a man in its jaws.

I thought I had come upon a novel illustration of Jonah, but am told that the legend here is that a bear threw these men into the sea, and the kind whales delivered them and brought them safe to land.

Talking of Jonah and the whale, reminds me of such a very neat story on that point, which I heard lately in Queensland, that I trust I may be forgiven for repeating it, hoping it may not prove a "Joe Miller" to many of my readers. The story is not only good in itself, but has the further advantage of "catching" most people, who almost invariably laugh at the wrong place and before the climax is reached. So much so indeed that I think a truly Christian person should mention this fact as a warning before telling the story.

It seems that on a certain occasion, a very shy young curate had elected to preach on the subject of Jonah being swallowed by a whale. It was a country congregation. The squire's pew was full of visitors, and amongst these was a foreign lady whose knowledge of English was rather limited.

"Jonah was three days in the whale's——" began the unfortunate young man—"in the whale's——." At length, with a desperate plunge, "*in the whale's*——*society !*"

Coming out of church the perplexed foreigner addressed herself to one of the gentlemen of the party.

"*Mais qu'est ce que ça veut dire donc? Qu'est ce que c'est que la société de la baleine?*" "The *society* of the whale?

madam," the gentleman answered with great presence of mind, " it means—a sort of *corporation*."

The village of Tongas consists of a few Indian houses, all closed up now as the inhabitants are off fishing and bringing down food for the winter season. Some beds of potatoes, turnips, &c. alone gave evidence that the desertion of the village was only temporary.

A good many old chiefs are buried here, and several wooden houses bore some such inscription as the following over them—

" In memory of (some unpronounceable Indian name), died 1880—aged 100 years." One inscription on a totem pole runs thus: " He died *at* his own hand."

After leaving Tongas, a heavy fog came on and delayed us for several hours.

The captain fired a gun continually, and by the length of time before the echo came he could alone judge of our distance from the rocks on either side, and so we steamed very slowly on.

And so the last day came, and passing once more through Queen Charlotte's Sound, we came alongside of Vancouver's Island, which lay now to our left.

After going to bed on the last night but one, a sudden stop came, and putting my head out of the window I found we had met another steamer of the company—the *Ancon*, just starting for the same expedition, two days out from Victoria.

There was much firing and saluting. They sent off a

boat for us to take back their mail and to send us news-papers from the civilized regions of Victoria.

The Driard Hotel, at the latter place, seemed a paradise of comfort when we reached it early on the morning of September 1st, just seventeen days since we had left its hospitable roof.

The Alaska expedition has much novelty to recommend it, and the beauty and wonders of Glacier Bay can scarcely be exaggerated. But so long as the world lasts, mental impressions must and will depend to a great extent upon physical conditions, and I think the Pacific Coast Steam Shipping Company might materially improve these latter by a little method and arrangement, to the greater comfort of the passengers and to their own abiding interest and advantage.

CHAPTER VIII.

OVER THE ROCKIES BY THE C.P.R.

TAKING a night boat from Victoria to the town of Vancouver,
on the mainland of British Columbia, we found ourselves
once more in that little township on the early morning of
Sunday, September 2nd.

Several of our fellow-passengers on the late Alaska trip
were with us, and I was much amused by the thorough
breakdown of their strictly Sabbatarian principles.

My friend and I, whose time was somewhat limited now,
had boldly announced our intention of taking the mid-day
train from Vancouver by the C.P.R. line to the east.

These good people looked very much shocked, and made a
great point of the fact that *they* would not travel on Sunday

but intended to remain over that day at Vancouver although at great inconvenience to themselves.

Arrived in Vancouver, they found on inquiry that no train for the east left on Monday. They must either travel on Sunday or remain until Tuesday.

The strain of the extra four-and-twenty hours proved too much for their principles, and every one of them came on in our train!

I do not know whether it was from my own stupidity or from the *couleur de rose* accounts of previous travellers, but my distinct impression had been that the *greater* portion of the C.P.R. Line was famous for its magnificent scenery.

This is a decided mistake, and I do not think anything is gained by misconception on such a point, as the traveller is only the more disappointed when he comes to prove matters by his own experience.

There is magnificent scenery on this line between Vancouver and Banff; that is to say, for the first thirty-six hours from the western terminus; but we must remember that at least ten hours of this is passed in darkness or such twilight as leaves little chance of seeing the scenery; whilst from Banff onwards there is nothing but the most depressing and melancholy prairie, as flat as a billiard-table and with absolutely no relief to the eye of the weary traveller.

It will however be always a favourite route, owing to the wonderful beauty of the Rocky Region whilst it lasts, and to Canada as a country it is impossible to exaggerate the advantages of possessing her own line of railway across this vast Continent.

She is now for the first time absolutely independent of American lines of rail for her passenger or commercial traffic, and, from a military point of view, would take a very different position now should there be any chance (which God forbid) of other than friendly relations between the two countries.

The C.P.R. Company have made a very good start in many ways.

Their carriages are well built, wider and more comfortable than any hitherto in use, and the restaurants placed at various points over the mountain route are exquisitely clean and inviting. The food is good in quality and well cooked, the linen and glass irreproachable. A deficiency of waiters is the only drawback. It is impossible for one miserable man to supply the wants of two large tables full of hungry travellers where only twenty to twenty-five minutes are allowed for dinner. It bade fair sometimes to be a case of starving in the sight of plenty, as the poor, overdriven man rushed wildly away to fulfil half-a-dozen orders, pursued by the plaintive reproaches of those still left unserved.

I noticed the same thing at all the stopping places, and on board the steamers of the C.P.R. (which take passengers who prefer that route to making the entire journey by land) the attendance was so bad that I have seen people leave the tables in despair after waiting for thirty or forty minutes in the vain hope of getting anything to eat.

We took this route ourselves, and the head steward was

most attentive and obliging, but powerless to do better with the
raw and insufficient " waiting " material given into his hands.
If economy is at the bottom of the nuisance, it is a very false
principle " to ruin the ship for want of a ha'porth of pitch,"
but probably the great difficulty of finding and keeping good
waiters on this Continent is the real reason for the one blot
on an otherwise excellent railway service.

The beauty of the scenery begins as soon as the train
leaves Vancouver, but the real magnificence of the Rocky
Mountain scenery comes after North Bend, which lies close
to the beautiful Fraser River.

Next morning we had left this behind, and passing several
large lakes to our left, notably the Great Shuswap Lake, and
crossing our old friend the Columbia River, we reached a
grand spot high up amongst the mountains where a wooden
look-out platform has been erected. The train stopped to
allow all passengers to alight and feast their eyes upon this
magnificent view.

Hundreds of feet sheer below us the water boiled and
surged, dashing through a narrow gorge, whilst trees which
had been uprooted by its force lay across and formed natural
bridges at intervals. The Rockies, grand and bare, rose up
on all sides and made one feel very small and insignificant
as we stood on this small square of wood overhanging the
precipice, and with nothing else between us and eternity.

The fires all along this line are very numerous, and the
blackened fir trees have a grim and desolate look.

Some of these fires are caused by lightning, and others

arc the result of intentional bush-clearing, whilst many arise from the carelessness of the men employed on the line who camp out in the forests.

As the train rises by a severe grade, crossing enormous ravines over colossal wooden viaducts of which the sweeping curves fascinate and yet terrify one, innumerable snow-sheds are passed on the mountain sides. These are very strongly built with iron clamps, but we passed the *débris* of more than one that had been literally *torn out of the ground* by the weight of the snows and rain, the iron clamps having been wrenched out like a row of so many pins!

The longest of these sheds (over a mile in length) is only used in winter; a summer track lying parallel with it.

Glacier Point, amidst the Selkirk mountains, was reached at lunch time on the second day of our journey. It is one of the most remarkable places on the route, and we had thought of halting for the night, but as no train leaves Vancouver on the Monday morning, this would have entailed losing our boat at Port Arthur, as we had arranged to make the trip of the lakes, which is a very pleasant change from the monotony of the train, and can only be undertaken with any pleasure during the two or three summer months.

So we made a very hasty meal, and spent most of our hour in watching the very dirty-looking but remarkable glacier, which rises quite clear above the little mountain inn, where very fair accommodation can be obtained by those wishing to break the journey here.

The view though magnificent is very much closed in, and I fancy the glacier would be a very difficult ascent, for it rises so abruptly and would entail a very hard climb.

A young man who came back from Sitka with us after spending three months in making a partial ascent of the famous Mount Elias, endorsed my opinion on this point, and as we looked upon his authority on such subjects as undeniable, we regretted the less being unable to stay here.

The mountain scenery becomes grander and grander as Glacier Point is left behind. The mountains themselves only average from three thousand to five thousand feet in height, but it is almost impossible to realize this, for they rise so sheer up from the plains, and one passes so close to them, that the tops seem almost to touch the skies. Unfortunately it was impossible to do more very often than *guess* at where the tops were, the mountains being so thickly enveloped in fog and smoke.

This natural atmospheric condition is much aggravated by the smoke of the numerous bush fires, so I fear most travellers must have a similar experience.

It was most tantalizing. Nevertheless we had a fine view of the "Kicking Horse" river, so called from the series of tiny rapids through which it swirls and rushes along.

Several young ladies of our party with their attendant swains, spent most of the day upon the "cow-catcher" and came back now and again, deep in coal black, but declaring they were having "a *lovely* time." I could quite believe it, and longed to join the party, but a special permission from a railway official is necessary, and owing doubtless to increasing illness, I had not sufficient energy left to procure this.

A third engine was chartered to take our heavy train up the incline, past the beautiful Kicking Horse Cañon, and by midnight we reached Banff, our resting-place for two nights; tired and hungry, but with firm faith in the boasted comforts of the new hotel there.

Alas for the vanity of human expectations! Not a crust of bread could be obtained, although this train brings in its freight of famished passengers every night.

"The steward goes to bed at 10 P.M." was the waiter's imperturbable answer to all inquiries and reproaches.

At length, after much cajoling, I persuaded a feeble-looking but good-natured underling to smuggle two pieces of bread and butter, and a small pint bottle of Bass into our rooms. Surely a loaf of bread and a little butter and beer might be left out in the interests of the nightly travellers, even if the steward *does* go to bed at ten o'clock.

Banff is situated at the eastern foot of the mountains, and is surrounded by them, but is far less shut in than Glacier Point, and hence has more variety of scenery than the latter place.

There is a small township of a few houses and stores, *four* churches (Roman Catholic, Presbyterian, American and English) and two doctors.

As Banff possesses hot sulphur springs and has already a Sanatorium, it is expected that it will shortly become a well-known and much-frequented mountain resort.

The Bow river flows through the valley here, and is very beautiful, having a " fall " on a small Niagara scale ; that is to say, very low, but broad and imposing.

The colouring of blue water is lovely ; soft green grey, turning into vivid green where the little " Spray " river flows into it.

The mountains look bleak and bare, having much uncovered lime formation up their rocky sides. We drove in the afternoon to one of the sulphur springs at the Sanatorium, about a mile or less from our hotel.

Here we found a large natural cave with a tiny circular hole at the top, through which the blue sky appeared. The depth of this circular sulphur spring is from four feet to six feet, and it was discovered accidentally by two young men, who saw the fumes arising out of the ground, and then came upon this lake down below.

The Sanatorium is a comfortable house, and many travellers prefer it to the more pretentious C.P.R. Hotel.

Three miles further up the mountain side, at a height of 800 feet, we came upon the Hot Springs settlement.

Here one large tank is built over the sulphur springs, and various small inns and wooden shanties have sprung up with bathing accommodation, and from hence iron pipes carry the water down to the Sanatorium.

I had a nasty accident here with our " buggy." The driver

told me to jump out when we arrived, but did *not* tell me of the brake rising up in the middle of the buggy and which was concealed by the folds of my gown. So I jumped and remained suspended in mid air, my arm being much bruised and severely strained by the poor man's valiant efforts to disengage the gown and lift me out. To add to our discomfort, a terrible hailstorm came on and we had to rattle home as best we could.

The views of the valley of the " Bow " and of the surrounding mountains would have been magnificent save for a heavy fog which, I imagine, is prevalent here.

Our driver declared that the thermometer went down to 60° below zero sometimes in the winter.

It is difficult to credit this, but of course a *dry* cold at that temperature might be easier to bear than our freezing point in the damp chill air of England.

A dull rainy day and my painful arm prevented our making a river expedition next day in a launch called the *Mountain Belle,* and we were quite reconciled to leaving Banff that evening in time to catch the night train on to Port Arthur. The dreary prairie country needs no comment. We had served an apprenticeship to this sort of thing in the " Far West " of America and resigned ourselves to books and meditation for the whole of the next day.

Having left Banff on Thursday night, we reached Port Arthur on the shores of Lake Superior on Saturday morning, and there took the steamer (*Athabasca*) for Owen's Sound, our landing-place on Lake Huron.

These steamers of the C.P.R. Company are fine, clean, and well fitted, with the one drawback already mentioned of very defective attendance.

A heavy storm came on soon after we embarked and drove us early to bed that night after a most ludicrous dinner scene, where plates, glasses and dishes flew about in hopeless confusion, to be shattered to pieces, owing to the absence of " fiddles " on the table.

The storms on these immense lakes are quite as severe and even more disagreeable than those on the ocean and should be guarded against as carefully.

Next day, at noon, we reached Sault St. Marie, the beautiful narrow straits and rapids dividing Lake Superior and Lake Huron, and quite the most picturesque spot on this lake trip.

In the afternoon also we passed some pretty lake scenery, and I divided my attention between admiring this and listening to a most interesting account of his travels given to me by a Mr. Williams, the young American I have already mentioned as having accompanied us back from Sitka.

He was one of a party of four men (two of them English) who had just made the only ascent yet achieved of the famous Mount Elias in Alaska. This mountain is 20,000 feet high, and two years ago Lieutenant Schwatka and Mr. Seton Karr made an attempt to ascend it.

It seems however that they only succeeded in climbing up 4,000 or 5,000 feet of a *spur* of the mountain, three or four miles away from the true ascent.

Seton Karr does not positively assert in his book that he

and Schwatka made the real ascent, but the inference is strong and rather calculated to mislead those ignorant of the facts and of the locality.

Mr. Williams and his three friends had to travel forty miles with "baggage Indians" and tents beyond the last Indian village from Sitka, where all civilization ceased.

They wasted eighteen days in making false attempts to scale the mountain, no trifling disaster where every pound of food had to be carried with them.

They were away twenty-eight days in all from Sitka and managed to ascend the cone of the mountain to a height of 12,000 feet, leaving a cairn to mark the spot reached, a precaution which Schwatka and Seton Karr seem to have neglected when climbing their spur.

Any future explorers will be able to save much time, profiting by this experience, and may hope to reach a greater height in consequence; for my friend and his companions were driven back chiefly through failure of provisions for a trip of such length of time.

A photographing apparatus had been taken, but something went wrong or the plates were smashed, and so Mr. Williams was forced to rely upon his pencil, and showed me some charming sketches of the mountain, giving the exact spot where the ascent was made, straight up towards the cone.[1]

On Monday we reached Toronto at noon, having disem-

---

[1] A very well written and charmingly illustrated article by Mr. Williams, describing the whole expedition, has appeared in *Scribner's Magazine* for April, 1889.

barked at Owen's Sound at 8 A.M. and coming on by
the tidal train.

Toronto was *en fête* that day, as the Exhibition was to be
opened at 2 P.M by Lord Stanley, the newly arrived Governor,
who was spending a few days in this town *en route* for
Ottawa, the Canadian seat of Government.

Next day I went to see the Exhibition with friends in the
city, and heard Lord Stanley read his congratulatory address
to the good citizens of Toronto.

All Exhibitions are very much alike, and so are most
addresses.

It is always "the proudest hour" in the life of the
Governor and of the people he has come out to govern.
Ça va sans dire.

Certainly my arrival in Toronto was not the proudest hour
or, at any rate, not the most fortunate hour in *my* life.

The terrible influenza caught in Alaska developed by
degrees into a serious and painful illness, and my last
association with Toronto is a nightmare of weary weeks in
bed and much pain and many doctors; but the heavy cloud
had the bright silver lining of tender sympathy and loving
care.

Of course the good people in England said "that comes
of foreign travel! We told you so!"

But illness is not confined to any climate nor to any
country.

As a rule, I am never in better health than when away
from my native shores. The English climate, taken all the

year round, is probably the most *liveable* climate in the world, but it is also one of the most depressing.

There is no more chance of breaking your leg in England than elsewhere, but there is far more chance of succumbing to atmospheric influences with their attendant evils, and I have always felt convinced that our gloomy, self-analysing and too often morbid religious convictions are a pure question of climate.

In any case, I have a strong theory that one gets nothing in this world without paying for it—in some way and at some time.

Thus I am fully resigned to have paid by weeks of ill health for my wider experiences, and for the many interesting friendships made and scenes beheld, since I steamed away from Plymouth in the good ship *Ionic* on my voyage round the world.

THE END.

RICHARD CLAY AND SONS, LIMITED, LONDON AND BUNGAY.

www.ingramcontent.com/pod-product-compliance
Lightning Source LLC
Chambersburg PA
CBHW020513270326
41926CB00008B/858